simply
REJOICING

12 Months with God

Patsy Lewis

BEACON HILL PRESS
OF KANSAS CITY

Printed in the
United States of America

Cover Design: Darlene Filley
Interior Design: Sharon Page

All Scripture quotations not otherwise designated are from the *Holy Bible, New Living Translation* (NLT), copyright © 1996, 2004, 2007 by Tyndale House Foundation. Used by permission of Tyndale House Publishers, Inc., Carol Stream, IL 60188. All rights reserved.

Permission to quote from the following copyrighted versions of the Bible is acknowledged with appreciation:

The *Holy Bible, English Standard Version*® (ESV®), copyright © 2001 by Crossway, a publishing ministry of Good News Publishers. Used by permission. All rights reserved.

The *New American Standard Bible*® (NASB®), © copyright The Lockman Foundation 1960, 1962, 1963, 1968, 1971, 1972, 1973, 1975, 1977, 1995.

The *Holy Bible, New International Version*® (NIV®). Copyright © 1973, 1978, 1984, 2011 by Biblica, Inc.™ Used by permission. All rights reserved worldwide.

The *New Revised Standard Version* (NRSV) of the Bible, copyright 1989 by the Division of Christian Education of the National Council of the Churches of Christ in the USA. Used by permission. All rights reserved.

The *Message* (TM). Copyright © 1993, 1994, 1995, 1996, 2000, 2001, 2002. Used by permission of NavPress Publishing Group.

Scripture quotations marked KJV are from the King James Version of the Bible.

Library of Congress Cataloging-in-Publication Data

Lewis, Patsy, 1942-
  Simply rejoicing : 12 months with God / Patsy Lewis.
    pages cm
  Includes bibliographical references.
  ISBN 978-0-8341-3093-7 (pbk.)
  1 God (Christianity)—Worship and love. 2. Spiritual life—Christianity. 3. Devotional literature. I. Title.
  BV4817.L49 2013
  242—dc23

2013030967

10 9 8 7 6 5 4 3 2 1

This book is dedicated to
my family,
who has awakened me to innumerable God moments!
To my husband, Curtis—my greatest supporter:
You have prayed, loved, and encouraged me through
every adventure that God has ordained.
To my children, Kevin and Lanissa—my God-given teachers:
You have taught me more than all my educators combined!
To my daughter-in-law, Michelle, and my son-in-law, Clay:
You are both special gifts to our family!
To my grandchildren:
Marissa, you are full of knowledge beyond your years!
Kiersten, you are capable of accomplishing
everything you set out to do!
Makaila, you fill hearts with joy and exuberance,
including mine!
Calvin, your depth of insight inspires me!
Caleb, your innovations both amaze and thrill me!
Laney, at age four,
you are already making an impact on the world!

CONTENTS

FOREWORD

I don't remember praying the prayer that touched my MiMi and inspired her to write her first book, *Simply Praying*. I have no memory of saying, "Jesus, I love you. I love you so much that I'm just going to run into your arms when I see you!"[1] But that's okay. I enjoy hearing about it from people who do remember, and I can certainly imagine myself running into the arms of Jesus when I see him.

When MiMi wrote *Simply Praying*, I was so excited. My own MiMi was an author! The book was extra-special to me, and I felt honored since it was inspired by my prayer and dedicated to me. There are billions of people in this world my MiMi could have chosen for the dedication of her book, but she chose me because of a four-year-old granddaughter's moving prayer that I don't remember.

All the chapter titles of *Simply Praying: 52 Weeks with God* begin with an action verb, titles like "Shadow Jesus," "Celebrate Daily," and "Remove the Baggage." These challenge the reader to a different prayer adventure every week.

MiMi's second book is called *Simply Listening: 12 Months with God*. It teaches the readers how to develop spiritual listening skills and hear messages from God.

This idea of a trilogy came to me while I was reading in my bed. I kept it to myself for a few days, thinking no one would listen to a twelve-year-old and her silly thoughts. Finally in an e-mail message to MiMi, I suggested she write a new book encouraging readers to watch for God in stories happening all around them. Although I originally suggested the title be *Simply Watching,* when we see God at work we can't help but simply rejoice. So here it is: *Simply Rejoicing,* a book that will lead you on a new adventure as you spend this year watching for God moments that will change your life forever!

—*Marissa Lewis*

PREFACE

My writing journey was a road I never expected to travel. In 2004 when Joyce Williams asked me to write for her book *She Can't Even Play the Piano!* she repeatedly said, "I want a chapter—but you have a book." I couldn't believe her, although others had encouraged me to write. I didn't think I had anything to say that hadn't already been written. At the beginning of 2005, however, it was clear that God was calling me to write a weekly prayer adventure. Without a publisher or professional direction, I set out to complete a chapter a week. Beacon Hill Press of Kansas City accepted my proposal and requested the manuscript by December, with release set for fall 2006. When the book *Simply Praying* was completed, I told my husband, Curtis, "I've written two books— my first and my last!" He would not accept that response and frequently asked when I planned to start the second book.

Once again I couldn't imagine that another book was forthcoming, yet in late 2007 I knew God was commissioning me to write *Simply Listening*. My plan was to write a section each month and have the manuscript completed by the end of 2008. I was stunned when I received an e-mail in early March requesting the manuscript by June. My home was sold in mid-March, a couple of days later my brother-in-law died suddenly of a heart attack, and I had a full spring speaking schedule. In the midst of moving, traveling, and family emergencies, I knew that if the book were to be finished by June, God would have to write it. He was faithful!

Book number three was birthed in November 2009 after the fourth "Come to the Fire" conference, a women's ministry for which I am prayer director. I have a host of prayer partners worldwide who pray for the readers of my books and my ministry. I send them a report after an event for which they have prayed. That early autumn morning following the conference, I awakened with the thought: *It would take a book to tell my prayer partners all that has happened the past three days.* Then I bolted upright in bed and said, "Oh, no!" Later that morning when I saw the conference director, Aletha Hinthorn, these words tumbled out: "I believe we're to write a book!" Within weeks *Come to the Fire Testimonies* was completed. A few days after that manuscript was sent to the publisher, I received an unexpected e-mail from my twelve-year-old granddaughter, Marissa, which prompted the writing of this book. It said—

Dear MiMi, I know that you are currently working on a book about experiences, but I have an idea. There is usually one book, a trilogy of books, etc. But see, I don't think I know any series of books that have only two books in them. I think you need to add one more book to your awesome "Simply" series. You have books on praying and listening, but why not have one on watching? You know, watching for miracles, seeing things through new eyes, seeing the Lord in everything you do, stuff like that. The books could be sold in trilogy packs, something bound to become popular. . . . It was just an idea that popped into my head a few nights ago, and I've been busting to share it ever since.

How would you respond to such a bold invitation from your pre-teen granddaughter? It was Marissa's prayer as a four-year-old that inspired the writing of *Simply Praying.* Her challenge to write yet another book caught me totally off guard much as her transparent preschool prayer had eight years before. I took her advice and began to watch more carefully than ever before, and daily God revealed himself in ways that I would have missed if I hadn't been watching. Seeing him at work all around me filled my days with rejoicing. My prayer is that God will use this book in your life, and if you also accept Marissa's exciting challenge to watch to see him at work around you, I am convinced this will be a year of rejoicing.

Simply Rejoicing is designed to be read slowly throughout the year, combined with suggested Scripture reading every month. Each of the twelve monthly sections is divided into two parts, the first to be read at the beginning of the month and the second at mid-month, with approximately two weeks allowed for reflection, soaking in the recommended scripture, and memorizing the suggested passage. If you follow the Bible reading plan, you'll have an overview of the life of Jesus and the miraculous work of his Holy Spirit in and through the early believers revealed in the New Testament. It's my prayer that as you read these biblical accounts and current-day God stories, you will be awakened to the work of the Holy Spirit, and your enhanced spiritual vision will send you forth to partner in God's miracles, simply rejoicing.

ACKNOWLEDGMENTS

I thank the God and Father of our Lord Jesus Christ, who through the power of the Holy Spirit brought about this work and daily shows me that he is here—all around me—everywhere if I simply watch with rejoicing.

My gratitude goes to Bonnie Perry, Gabriele Udell, and the entire Beacon Hill Press team who covered all details and creatively made this project happen.

I am indebted to the great crowd of witnesses, family and friends, who encouraged and prayed for me throughout the writing of *Simply Rejoicing*.

It is with great joy that I share the miracles of God at work all around us from dear ones who permitted me to include their stories in these chapters: Jane Berry, Bud Preston, Loyd Olsan, Jenny Jordan, Yori Taylor, Eve Soulain, Wanda Garrett, Bonnie Cash, Tina Mitchell, Julie Arbuckle, and other friends anonymously as well as my supportive family—Kevin, Michelle, Marissa, Kiersten, and Makaila Lewis; Lanissa, Clay, Calvin, Caleb, and Laney Brantley; and my faithful husband and cheerleader, Curtis.

INTRODUCTION

A moment can change your life forever. A brief encounter, what seemed like a routine activity, an event that you thought would be ordinary, can become a transformational dot in time. I will never be the same after hearing my four-year-old granddaughter Marissa's ten–second prayer that inspired me to write *Simply Praying*. It took less than a half minute to read the surprising e-mail I received from her eight years later encouraging me to write another book in the "Simply" series. I asked God if this could be his way of getting a message to me and received confirmation.

In my listening times the next week, he began to advise me to move forward with blind faith, but not to plunge in too quickly. Interestingly, he admonished me to be alert at all times, to watch, wait, listen, and record what he revealed to me daily. Three days before I received Marissa's unexpected e-mail, I recorded the following scripture in my journal, writing the full verses in more than one translation: "Pay close attention to what you hear. The closer you listen, the more understanding you will be given—and you will receive even more" (Mark 4:24). "Then pay attention to how you listen; for to those who have, more will be given" (Luke 8:18, NRSV). It could be restated as "To those who listen to my teaching, more understanding will be given" (Luke 8:18).

I pondered the "pay attention" phrase, believing that God was inviting me to be alert to something. I began to watch and listen with expectancy, never dreaming that several hours later I would open an e-mail that would catapult me into a new God-sized adventure.

I'm learning that watching is more than optical vision. It means to pay attention, to take notice and be aware with all senses heightened. When a mother shouts, "Watch out!" to a small child, she may mean stop and proceed with caution because she hears a panting dog, smells garbage, or senses other danger. Watching involves intention, alertness, attentiveness, observation, scrutiny, analysis. It may heighten anticipation, cause us to examine details, lead us to notice things we would otherwise miss, make us aware of surroundings, or alert us to search for cause and effect. Spiritually watching entices us to read the Word carefully, to pray with a discerning spirit, and to go about our day with holy anticipation, rejoicing at each discovery.

Rejoicing implies alertness, attentiveness, and involvement as well as energy, activity, and participation. Throughout this book I am emphasizing watching with the expectation that the by-product will be great rejoicing.

I extend Marissa's invitation to you to watch to see where God is at work in your world. No doubt you will observe miracles others may miss. Perhaps he will ask you to write or tell his story as it is revealed through your journey with him. Believe me—a book, a prayer, an e-mail, a scripture, a moment with God can change your life eternally! Read prayerfully, simply rejoicing with each insight he reveals.

ARISE AND EXALT YOUR CREATOR

I. AWAKEN WITH PRAYER

A "Trinity Sunrise Prayer" can alter your perspective today!

In the beginning God created the heavens and the earth. . . . Then God looked over all he had made, and he saw that it was very good! (Genesis 1:1, 1:31).

....

Each morning I pray my "Trinity Sunrise Prayer":
I am rising today in the name of the Father
who created me,
sent his Son to redeem me,
watches over me,
and hears my prayers.
Heavenly Father, may I behold the wonders of your creation throughout
this day and see through your eyes and heart the world around me and
everyone you choose to cross my path.
I am rising today in the name of the Son,
who gave his life for me,
has forgiven my sins,
understands my suffering,
and loves me.

Precious Jesus, may I exalt you in all that I do and say, and may my lips praise you with a heart of thanksgiving for your blessings and saving grace.

I am rising today in the name of the Holy Spirit,

who breathed life into me

and lives in my heart.

Breath of heaven, breathe afresh on me today, and may I be aware of your presence every waking moment and even as I lie down to rest at the end of the day.

Holy God, Three in One, Father, Son, and Holy Spirit, I commit this day to you.

Saying this Trinity Sunrise Prayer each morning changes the way I view my day and gives me an alertness I otherwise wouldn't have. Actually, I prayed this prayer five hours before sunrise this morning. I awakened at about 2:00 A.M., coughing and mind racing. When I was unable to go back to sleep, I went to another room to pray, read the Word, and write. The sun has been up for hours now, but I have not seen it because of the heavy cloud cover. It is five days before Christmas, and I know that the light of the Son whose birthday we are celebrating is with me today although dark clouds are hovering.

I attended the funeral of a forty-two-year-old family friend who died of a massive heart attack, no forewarning, leaving three children behind. My husband is at the hospital intensive care unit with a dear gentleman from our church who is critically ill, not expected to live to see Christmas. I spent an hour this morning with a young mother who had a heart attack a couple of weeks ago. My son-in-law is traveling four hours to his aunt's funeral today. With all these sad circumstances and more swirling around me, my sunrise prayer has changed my perspective on it all.

I admit it isn't unusual for me to doze off or for my mind to wander as I pray this morning prayer; however, God knows that I am deeply sincere in my request for a daily fresh outpouring of his Spirit and desire to behold, exalt, and commit. I was prompted to write my Trinity Sunrise Prayer several years ago by a suggestion in one of Calvin Miller's publications on prayer.[1] Praying this prayer for the past six years has never become a ritual. It reminds me daily that as mysterious as the Trinity is to me, the one true God reveals himself in Scripture as Father, Son, and Holy Spirit, and I, God's created being, am impacted by these three divine, interrelated personalities.

Then God said, "Let us make man in our image, after our likeness" (Genesis 1:26, ESV). *Then the LORD God formed man from the dust of the ground. He breathed the breath of life into the man's nostrils, and the man became a living person* (Genesis 2:7).

John 1:1-14 speaks of Jesus and his participation in creation: *In the beginning was the Word, and the Word was with God, and the Word was God. He was with God in the beginning. Through him all things were made; without him nothing was made that has been made* (John 1:1-3, NIV).

This living Word, Jesus, became the visible God when he came to earth fully God, yet fully man.

The Word became flesh and made his dwelling among us (John 1:14, NIV).

No one has ever seen God. But the unique One, who is himself God, is near the Father's heart. He has revealed God to us (John 1:18).

In *The Heart of the Gospel* Robert Coleman calls this Jesus "the photograph of God."[2]

The first reference to the Spirit in the Bible is in chapter one of Genesis; verse two says that the "Spirit of God was hovering over the waters." From the very beginning we see the relationship of Father, Son, and Spirit participating in creation. Among other places in Scripture, the holy three persons are mentioned at the baptism of Jesus[3] and are named when Jesus gave his great commission to his disciples.[4] Jesus proclaimed the promise of the outpoured Spirit and explained the work of the Spirit to his disciples at his last meal with them,[5] and his final words in Luke's Gospel are—

And now I will send the Holy Spirit, just as my Father promised. But stay here in the city until the Holy Spirit comes and fills you with power from heaven (Luke 24:49).

The Holy Trinity isn't easy for the human mind to comprehend. Although many faulty attempts have been made to explain it, Robert Coleman writes, "God is beyond us as the Father, among us as the Son, and within us as the Spirit."[6] Ultimately Coleman says, "All . . . efforts to explain the Trinity of God . . . cannot adequately describe the Godhead. . . . But the wonder of it causes a wise person to reverence even more the greatness of God."[7]

I believe in the greatness of God even with my unanswered questions. He is my creator who watches over me and both hears and answers my prayers. I want to rise each day in awe of his majestic world, see in every person I meet his or her potential for glorifying his or her maker, and rejoice that the Father sent his Son to redeem me.

In the midst of the sadness I'm facing today, I believe in God's love, which is demonstrated through the life of his Son, who willingly obeyed the Father and gave his life for me. This Savior has forgiven my sins and, because of his great suffering while on earth, fully understands my pain. The Cross reminds me of his lavish love outpoured for me.

Although I cannot see him, the Holy Spirit surrounds and comforts me. He breathes fresh life into me daily. I am thrilled that I awakened today with prayer communicating with Father, Son, and Holy Spirit, and it's a perfect way to end the day.

A few weeks ago as I was praying with and saying good-night to my granddaughter Marissa, she abruptly asked, "MiMi, what are your favorite three quotes?" She caught me off guard, so I asked her to share hers while I thought for a moment. She quickly recited three, including "Today is the tomorrow you worried about yesterday." Then she added two others that she observed on posters hanging in her room.

It was now my turn. I told her that I have a piece of framed art etched with words that were found scratched on a wall in Germany in 1945 believed to be written by someone during the Holocaust. It is a profound statement of faith in the midst of adversity that I claim for myself:

I believe in the sun even when it is not shining;

in love even when I am alone;

and in God even when he is silent.

In spite of gray skies, agonizing grief, and unanswered questions of this day, I see evidence of God at work, and I believe! At the funeral today a soloist sang "Turn Your Eyes upon Jesus," and the minister turned our focus toward Jesus. This is my vision for every reader of *Simply Rejoicing*: that as we look to Jesus in Scripture, we will see evidence of his Spirit at work daily, and no matter what clouds may be obscuring our view of God, we will behold, believe, commit, and rejoice.

I invite you to return to my Trinity Sunrise Prayer and pray it for yourself, that you will behold God's creation, see through his eyes and heart those he allows to cross your path, exalt Jesus as you find him at work in your world, be aware of the Holy Spirit's presence surrounding you, and acknowledge blessings throughout your day, rejoicing and believing that the one true God—Father, Son, and Holy Spirit—will reveal himself to you from the moment you arise until day's end.

Reflections

- I encourage you to keep a journal of revelations during your *Simply Rejoicing* journey and to read the recommended scripture with a prayerful attentive heart and mind, recording new insights and blessings.
- Write your own Trinity Sunrise Prayer.

- For the next fifteen days, make a list of ways you see God at work; then say a prayer rejoicing for his intervention in your world.

How I See God at Work

Day 1 _____

Day 2 _____

Day 3 _____

Day 4 _____

Day 5 _____

Day 6 _____

Day 7 _____

Day 8 _____

Day 9 _____

Day 10 _____

Day 11 _____

Day 12 _____

Day 13 _____

Day 14 _____

Day 15 _____

Scripture

Before continuing to Part II for this month, read prayerfully and with alertness Genesis 1; John 1:1-34; and Colossians 1. Then begin reading the Gospel of Luke, looking at the life of Jesus, absorbing his teachings, and examining his miracles. Take time to ponder the lessons he has for you to discover.

Memorize John 1:14 (NIV)

The Word became flesh and made his dwelling among us. We have seen his glory, the glory of the one and only Son, who came from the Father, full of grace and truth.

Suggestion

Begin with one phrase, and when it is memorized add another.

Reflection Insights

_____

_____

_____

_____

_____

_____

_____

_____

_____

_____

_____

_____

_____

_____

_____

_____

_____

_____

_____

_____

_____

_____

II. TURN YOUR FOCUS TOWARD JESUS

New insight can help you refocus your spiritual goals!

> *At that same time Jesus was filled with the joy of the Holy Spirit, and he said, "O Father, Lord of heaven and earth, thank you for hiding these things from those who think themselves wise and clever, and for revealing them to the childlike. Yes, Father, it pleased you to do it this way. My Father has entrusted everything to me. No one truly knows the Son except the Father, and no one truly knows the Father except the Son and those to whom the Son chooses to reveal him." Then when they were alone, he turned to the disciples and said, "Blessed are the eyes that see what you have seen"* (Luke 10:21-23).

As I write this, it is the third day of January, and my theme for the new year is "Watching." In mid-October I asked God if he had a plan to give me for writing a book on watching him at work around me, and I began to scribble goals for myself. I sensed that I wanted to spend time each day in prayer focused on the book. A couple of days later during my listening time, God called me into an extended time apart with him. This period of prayer and listening resulted in four main goals:

Goal One: My number-one personal goal is *to keep my relationship with my Creator fresh through prayer and communication with him.* This will include not only a Trinity Sunrise Prayer, my listening times, and prayer over this book, but also other avenues in prayer that God unfolds.

While prayerfully listening for God's message to me December 19, I wrote—*I'm not through teaching you all about prayer that I want you to know. The book you will be writing is as much for you as it is for the readers who will come to know me better and see me through new eyes of understanding. Mysteries will be revealed.*

Goal Two: Another goal I have for this year is *to read the New Testament in chronological order,* searching for all the times the reader or listener is warned to watch or encouraged to rejoice.

During the Christmas season I wanted to read about the life of Jesus and chose to read the four Gospels meshed together in what is perhaps the timeline of his teachings and miracles. A few days before Christmas I read the Gospel of Luke, paying careful attention to all the places Jesus cautioned his listeners to pay attention, watch, or observe something closely. I selected Luke because it includes the birth of Jesus and walks the reader through his life, ministry, death, resurrection, and ascension.

I am now rereading Luke slowly—probing, digging, exploring, and attempting to put myself into each scene asking questions: "What do you see, Patsy?" "How does it feel to see Jesus at work around you?" "How would you be rejoicing at such a miracle?"

Goal Three: This leads to my next goal, which is *to watch throughout my day to see Jesus at work in my world*—to turn my eyes and focus toward the Son, allowing him to continue to reveal truth to me as a result of my quiet time of listening and prayerfully reading the Word!

Yesterday I received new insight while reading a biblical story that I love. I've often paused at the question Jesus asked the blind beggar who called out, "Son of David, have mercy on me!" (Luke 18:39). Frequently he asks me the same question: "What do you want me to do for you?" (Luke 18:41).

At 4:30 A.M. yesterday I bolted upright in my recliner when I read the blind man's response at the end of that verse: "Lord," he said, "I want to see!" That's exactly what I've been saying and fervently expressed that desire again: "I want to see!" Then I knew the Master was asking me a new question: "Patsy, what do you want to see?" I felt that he expected a response, and I immediately wrote, "I want to see you—to see your glory revealed. I want to behold the wonder of your creation—to see divine miracles. I want to see truth in Scripture that I may have missed previously." And my list continues as I turn my eyes toward Jesus.

This morning I went back to that story in Luke 18:35-43 and read verses 42-43:

And Jesus said, "All right, receive your sight! Your faith has healed you." Instantly the man could see, and he followed Jesus, praising God. And all who saw it praised God, too.

This is how I picture it: As we turn our focus toward Jesus and tell him what we want to see, he honors our desire by giving divine sight. Then, as we in faith follow him and give God praise, others no doubt will be watching and will join us in praising and rejoicing!

Goal Four: I have one additional goal to share—*to read a book each week.* I have been praying for God to reveal books that he wants referenced in *Simply Rejoicing.* Before Christmas, Curtis and I received *The Heart of the Gospel,* by Robert E. Coleman, as a gift from the Francis Asbury Society, and I am enjoying digging into it slowly. This is the first book that I believe was sent as an answer to my specific prayer.

Another book came a few days ago from my husband. It is not unusual for Curtis to read one or more books a week, and after purchasing his newest publication, he enthusiastically invited me to read it. I eagerly began turning pages January 1 and read the final page January 2. I couldn't put the book down, and *The Circle Maker,* by Mark Batterson, is now included in my list of favorite books.

During my quiet reflection time December 5, I was sure God was challenging me to pray bold prayers, and I wrote his message:

Do not lift half-hearted prayers to me. Pray bold prayers, in faith, not wavering or doubting. This is my invitation to you.

I was wide-eyed as I read the following words in Batterson's book: "Bold prayers honor God, and God honors bold prayers."[1] I embraced what Batterson said next: "God isn't offended by your biggest dreams or boldest prayers. He is offended by anything less. If your prayers aren't impossible to you, they are insulting to God. Why? Because they don't require divine intervention."[2]

Turn your eyes toward Jesus in Luke's gospel, and you will discover him divinely intervening, doing the impossible, casting out demons, healing many afflictions, raising dead people, calming storms, feeding multitudes, forgiving sinners, transforming lives, and fulfilling Old Testament prophecies. This same Jesus modeled prayer; he taught his disciples to ask and invited them to join him in prayer.

Batterson says, "Prayers are prophecies. They are the best predictors of your spiritual future. *Who you become* is determined by *how you pray.* Ultimately, the transcript of your prayers becomes the script of your life."[3] Wow! Batterson has a life goal list and says, "Goal-setting begins and ends with prayer."[4] In his steps to goal-setting he includes these: start with prayer, check your motives, be specific, write it down, celebrate along the way, dream big, and pray hard.[5]

I invite you to reread Batterson's quote in the above paragraph and then pause to pray a bold prayer, refocus, and turn your eyes toward Jesus. As you look to Jesus for new insight, he will fill your eyes and heart with light, help you refocus your spiritual goals, and give you meaningful plans that will exalt him!

Reflections

Before you move forward to the second month in your journey through *Simply Rejoicing*, I recommend that you pause for a couple of weeks to do prayerful goal-setting for the year.

- Ask God what he wants to accomplish through you and how you can exalt him.
- Record your goals and read them daily, rejoicing with each accomplishment.

My Goals

_____

_____ __

_____

_____

_____

_____

Scripture

Read the entire Gospel of Luke. Covering two chapters a day, you will finish the book in twelve days.

Memorize Luke 11:34

Your eye is a lamp that provides light for your body. When your eye is good, your whole body is filled with light. But when it is bad, your body is filled with darkness.

Suggestion

Write Luke 11:34 on a card to prop beside a lamp that you use frequently. Each time you turn the lamp on or off, reread the card; then look away and say as much of the verse as you can recall.

Reflection Insights

LISTEN AND CRAVE TIME WITH YOUR SAVIOR

I. FAST WITH EYES OPEN

A fast may alert you to future temptation.

Then Jesus, full of the Holy Spirit, returned from the Jordan River. He was led by the Spirit in the wilderness, where he was tempted by the devil for forty days. Jesus ate nothing all that time and became very hungry. Then the devil said to him, "If you are the Son of God, tell this stone to become a loaf of bread." But Jesus told him, "No! The Scriptures say, 'People do not live by bread alone'" (Luke 4:1-4).

Caleb, our grandson, was a toddler the first time he volunteered to say table grace before eating and boldly enforced his "eyes open" rule. He would look at everyone intently as he said, "Eyes open," making sure that all were complying with his command. Then he would pray his "God is great; God is good; now I thank him for this food" blessing. Caleb, like his MiMi and most other people I know, loves food.

It's true—I love to eat! When I cook a meal, I'm tempted to eat three times. Usually I sample the food while preparing it, sit down and eat a serving from every dish, then "clean up" the leftovers as I take care of the mess. The taste of food isn't all that I enjoy about eating. I inhale the aromas, appreciate the textures, praise a beautiful presentation, and delight in fellowship when sharing a meal with others.

Last week at a church fellowship a lady brought a beautiful tray of sandwiches. When I commented about how attractive her dishes always are, she replied, "We eat with our eyes first." Yes, I feast on food not only with sight and taste but with all my senses; even the sounds of food preparation excite me.

This love affair with food makes it difficult for me to fast. I confess—all I seem to think about is food. Questions bombard my mind as I read about Jesus fasting in the wilderness before he began his public ministry. How did he do it? He was human—he was hungry; he was tempted! I want to learn everything possible from the life of Jesus in this arena of fasting and temptation.

It seems clear to me that temptation isn't sin. Jesus was full of the Holy Spirit, doing exactly what the Spirit led him to do. The Scripture makes it evident that the enemy doesn't give up bombarding us with temptation, because Luke reports that the devil tempted Jesus for forty days and then left until the next opportunity came.[1] How did Luke know this unless Jesus told someone of his experience in the wilderness? Perhaps he shared with his disciples about his temptations when he was giving them warnings.

Jesus made it clear that temptations are inevitable (see Matthew 18:7) and implied that his disciples would face temptation as he taught them to pray, "And don't let us yield to temptation" (Luke 11:4). When they were sleeping in the garden of Gethsemane he warned them, "Get up and pray so that you will not give in to temptation" (Luke 22:46).

From Jesus I want to learn how to be alert for temptation, face it when it confronts me without forewarning, and resist all enemy attacks. To explain the meaning of the parable of the seed, Jesus said, "The seeds on the rocky soil represent those who hear the message and receive it with joy. But since they don't have deep roots, they believe for a while, then they fall away when they face temptation" (Luke 8:13). How do we get deep roots? What makes it possible for us to withstand temptation? From Jesus' example in the wilderness, I'm suspecting that fasting, spending time alone with God, praying, and quoting scripture are key ingredients.

I'll be up front with you—I'm not a good faster and am no authority on the subject, but if I follow Jesus' example, I will fast. When the Pharisees and teachers of religious law complained to Jesus that his disciples did not fast, Jesus responded in his picturesque way: "Do wedding guests fast while celebrating with the groom? Of course not. But someday the groom will be taken away from them, and then they will fast" (Luke 5:34-35). Jesus seemed to be saying that his disciples would fast when he was no longer with them. Interestingly, this discussion on fasting appears just verses after Levi held a banquet with Jesus as the honored guest.[2]

It's no secret that Jesus loved to eat. He was criticized for eating with sinners. He fed multitudes. Martha prepared a big dinner for him. He told parables about food. His last night with his disciples was celebrated with a meal, and he fed them breakfast after his resurrection. It isn't wrong to enjoy food; otherwise, we wouldn't be nourished and thrive. So what is the purpose of fasting? Why do we fast? When do we fast?

Once again, let's turn our eyes toward Jesus. Like Jesus, we fast when the Spirit leads us. We fast when facing a challenging ministry. In Matthew 6:16-18 Jesus warned not to fast as hypocrites do, to impress others and be seen as spiritual. This warning immediately follows the Lord's Prayer and Jesus' teaching on prayer. Biblical fasting is not for the purpose of weight loss, to cleanse the body, or to perform a legalistic ritual. Its primary purpose is prayer.

I'm rereading portions of Elmer L. Towns' book *Fasting for Spiritual Breakthrough*. This book is filled with insight on fasting—how to prepare, what to expect, precautions to take, various kinds of fasts, biblical examples, and promised blessings. Towns says, "Although I do not think fasting is mandatory for believers today, I do believe the discipline is available to strengthen you spiritually and to help you overcome barriers that might keep you from living the victorious Christian life."[3] However, he is convinced—"If every Christian fasted, the results could shake our society like a windstorm bending a sapling. Christians would demonstrate that they live differently, that their faith is imperative, that the Almighty works in their daily lives."[4]

Towns warns that when you fast, "you can expect resistance, interference and opposition. Plan for it, insofar as you are able. Do not be caught unawares."[5] He reminds us that we are attempting "to gain ground for the kingdom . . . and no great movement of the Holy Spirit goes unchallenged by the enemy."[6]

There are numerous reasons for entering a fast; however, it is imperative that it be for the right motive and only when God has called you to it.

This week I joined a large group of Christian leaders for a three-day prayer-and-fasting convocation. During the noon break the third day, Jim held up his water bottle to his adult son, Doug, and jokingly said, "Want to share my lunch?" With a broad smile, Doug held up his own water bottle and joyfully said, "Thanks—I have mine." The conversation then proceeded to scripture about living water and Jesus' invitation to drink.

Nancy, a full-time intercessor, commented that it is easier to fast with a group and no kitchen or food nearby. I was a weakling among champions of fasting. I admit I ate my oatmeal or cereal each morning and kept my English walnuts with me—just in case; however, I found it to be true that it was easier to fast jointly with a group for a common purpose. Several, who for health reasons could not do a total fast, chose other options, denying themselves of various things to show their earnestness and dependence upon God.

Recently when I was in the midst of a forty-day partial fast with thousands of other Christians, God called me apart with him for an extended time, not to the wilderness for forty days but to a twenty-four-hour silent prayer retreat. This was my second quiet retreat. My first ran from Good Friday afternoon to the evening before Easter, which was a perfect season to be alone with God. My second silent retreat eight years later came two weeks before Christmas. I knew the purpose for which God was calling me to come away with him. It was not to prepare for the beginning of my public ministry, as with Jesus, but to fortify me for the continuation of his calling on my life. This also follows the example of Jesus.

After the wilderness experience, I find Jesus in the Gospels often going to a place of quiet solitude to be alone with the Father. I think of it as Father, Son, and Spirit communing. Intimacy and communication with the Father were his secret for withstanding temptation, and it is mine and yours as well.

A silent retreat is not necessarily accompanied by fasting from food—neither of mine was. It is a fast from talking and noise and the hurry-scurry of distractions for the purpose of listening and fellowship with your Maker and Redeemer. It may include reading the Bible and other Christian literature, walking and observing God's handiwork, even sleeping and getting needed rest. Looking back, I have discovered that my first silent retreat came as I was launching a new major prayer ministry and prior to writing my books on prayer. At that time I had no idea what God had in store, but as I sat in a rocking chair on the porch of a small log cabin overlooking the beautiful hills and landscape of the conference center, he spoke softly into my heart, telling me to walk forward into the plan he was unfolding step by step. It was a holy moment too precious to convey. He began swinging doors open and has continued.

The purpose of my second silent retreat was to prepare my heart for Christmas and for writing this book, plus other avenues of ministry he is orchestrating. I must be alert, fortified, and empowered for each assignment he ordains. Jesus is my example; it is my desire to exalt him and be on guard for temptations that may creep into the picture.

Although food was not the only temptation Jesus faced in the wilderness, it was the first. Almost every person I know is facing an eating issue—being overweight or underweight, dealing with food addictions or food allergies. A few months ago little five-year-old Caleb, who has battled asthma and ear infections, was diagnosed with multiple food and non-food allergies. I don't know anyone who loves sweets more than my ninety-five-year-old mother, who has diabetes. The granddaughter of a lady in our church was recently hospitalized for anorexia. A friend sent a request to pray for her husband who leads a major ministry and as a result of health issues needs to gain weight. I have other friends battling a variety of food disorders.

Food and related issues often dominate our thoughts and lives. Of course, food is essential for sustained life but frequently tempts us to misuse it. Since Jesus, too, was tempted with food, he can point us to ways of overcoming this and all other temptations. By quoting scripture, Jesus overcame the enemy's temptation to use his divine power to turn stones into bread.

Jesus' weapon against temptation was time alone with the Father, fasting, praying, and quoting God's Word at each temptation. Obviously he had fed on Scripture, digested it, and was strengthened and fortified by its nourishment. Scripture was so much a part of who he was that he effortlessly quoted exactly the right passage at each temptation. I, too, want to devour the Word so that I will be alert to cravings that are not healthful and will be able to quote scripture in the face of temptation. One way I am doing this is to commit passages to memory, and I am inviting you to join me by memorizing a verse at the end of each chapter of *Simply Rejoicing.*

Lysa TerKeurst, president of Proverbs 31 Ministries, uses ninety-nine Scripture passages in her book *Made to Crave.* The subtitle of her *New York Times* bestseller is *Satisfying Your Deepest Desire with God, Not Food.* She says, "We crave what we eat."[7] Could it be true that we crave Scripture more and more as we read it, ponder it, memorize it, chew on it, and digest its food? It's beneficial to read the Word with eyes and heart open for its truth in order to be alert for temptation and equipped when it attacks.

Following the forty days in the wilderness, Luke relates that Jesus then returned to Galilee "filled with the Holy Spirit's power" (Luke 4:14). When he came to his hometown of Nazareth, he opened the scroll in the synagogue and read from the prophet Isaiah: "The Spirit of the LORD is upon me, for he has anointed me to preach Good News to the poor. He has sent me to proclaim that captives will be released, that the blind will see, that the oppressed will be set free, and that the time of the LORD's favor has come" (Luke 4:18-19). Then he proclaimed, "The Scripture you've just heard has been fulfilled this very day!" (Luke 4:21).

Luke moves from that scene to his first recorded miracle of Jesus—casting out a demon. Although those in Nazareth would not accept Jesus, the demon shouted, "I know who you are—the Holy One of God!" (Luke 4:34).

This Holy One sent from God is our visible image of God, the one we are to look toward for facing temptation victoriously and moving forward in ministry with the power of his Holy Spirit.

We may bow our head and close our eyes to pray, but eating and fasting are to be done with eyes open—alert to enemy intrusion, prepared to face temptation with Scripture and thus mobilized to minister with Spirit anointing and power!

Reflections

- During the next two weeks, set aside a few hours for a silent retreat, spending time with Jesus and listening for any messages he may have for you. Examples: 7:00 P.M. to 7:00 A.M. one night, 2:00 P.M. to 5:00 P.M. Sunday afternoon, a Saturday morning, or a full twenty-four hours.
- Fast and pray as the Holy Spirit invites you.

Scripture

Read John 13-17, watching for all references to the Spirit.

Memorize 1 Corinthians 10:12-13

If you think you are standing strong, be careful not to fall. The temptations in your life are no different from what others experience. And God is faithful. He will not allow the temptation to be more than you can stand. When you are tempted, he will show you a way out so that you can endure.

Suggestion

- Repeat the scripture above, paraphrasing it in your own words.

1 Corinthians 10:12-13 in My Own Words:

_____

_____

_____

_____

_____

_____

_____

_____

- Turn it into a prayer of affirmation: *God, you are faithful! No matter how great my temptation becomes, you, the powerful One, will help me endure it.*
- Write the scripture on a card to carry in your pocket. Read it at every opportunity until you can quote it without hesitation at the first inkling of temptation.

Reflection Insights

II. FOLLOW THE MASTER

A word from your Creator will enlarge your vision!

> *By his divine power, God has given us everything we need for living a godly life. We have received all of this by coming to know him, the one who called us to himself by means of his marvelous glory and excellence. And because of his glory and excellence, he has given us great and precious promises. These are the promises that enable you to share his divine nature and escape the world's corruption caused by human desires* (2 Peter 1:3-4).

No one in Bud's family went to church or even talked about religion. When he started school, it was there that he heard there was a God. About the age of seven while lying in a grassy field one sunny day, he looked into the brilliant blue sky and said, "They tell me there's a God; if there is, where are you?" He immediately heard this clear response: *I'm here! I'm all around you! I'm everywhere!* Bud reflected as he told his story to me: "Although the voice was not audible, it was very real. I can hear it as clearly today as I could then." That was fifty-plus years ago.

Bud also heard at school that you could learn about God in the Bible, but no one he knew owned one. One day he discovered a small New Testament at his grandmother's, and he stole it. He would sneak to read it until the day his father discovered his secret and told him to return it with an apology to his grandmother. In the presence of his father, she gave the Bible to Bud as a gift.

He was a young adult before he moved from the country to town and lived near a church, and by the time he gave his heart to Jesus, he had become involved in unwholesome activities and formed destructive habits. He testifies that the day he received Christ into his life, it was as if he entered the church doors from a world of black and white but came out to a world of vivid, living color. He was transformed and passionately endeavored to set the world ablaze for God.

Eventually Bud became weary in his Christian efforts and made a visit to his pastor. In defeat he said, "I quit!"

The pastor replied, "You can't," explaining to Bud that it's impossible to live the Christian life in one's own strength. To be a victorious Christ-follower, a believer must commit all to God, fully surrendered, embracing obedience while allowing the Holy Spirit to cleanse, empower, and guide.

Bud, like the New Testament apostle Simon Peter, had hit a wall. Among Jesus' first and final recorded words to Simon was this invitation: "Follow me."[1] When Jesus summoned Simon, the fisherman willingly obeyed and left his fishing boat to follow Jesus. It was after a night of prayer that Jesus chose his apostles. The Synoptic Gospels, Matthew, Mark, and Luke, all place Simon's name first on the list of twelve.[2] Jesus gave him the name "Cephas" in Aramaic, "Peter" in Greek, which means "rock."[3] In giving Simon a new name, it is clear that the Master saw potential in Peter.

Simon Peter watched Jesus provide a miraculous catch of fish, heal his mother-in-law, calm the storm, and feed the multitudes. Along with the other apostles, he was given the power to cast out demons and heal diseases.[4] Peter briefly walked on water to Jesus[5] and on another occasion boldly proclaimed, "You are the Messiah, the Son of the living God" (Matthew 16:16). When many followers were deserting Jesus, Peter affirmed his faith, answering Jesus' question to the twelve, "Are you also going to leave?" Simon Peter replied, "Lord, to whom would we go? You alone have the words that give eternal life. We believe them, and we know you are the Holy One of God" (John 6:67-69). In spite of witnessing these wondrous acts and making public affirmations of belief in Jesus, Peter had frailties.

Although Jesus knew Peter's weaknesses, he had a greater vision and purpose for his life. Jesus gave him the special privilege, along with James and John, of witnessing several phenomenal events, including the raising of Jairus's daughter[6] and the transfiguration.[7] In the story of the transfiguration, a verse that haunts me is Luke 9:32. Peter fell asleep as Jesus prayed on the mountain. He dozed and almost missed the glorious revelation. It reminds me that we can be close to glory and miss it—sleep through it.

Again Peter slept in the Garden of Gethsemane when Jesus took him along with James and John into the olive grove. Jesus told them, "My soul is crushed with grief to the point of death. Stay here and keep watch with me" (Mark 14:34). Yet he agonized in prayer alone. When he found the disciples sleeping, he said to Peter, "Simon, are you asleep? Couldn't you watch with me even one hour? Keep watch and pray, so that you will not give in to temptation. For the spirit is willing, but the body is weak" (Mark 14:37-38).

How did Peter miss it? He was warned to watch! When Jesus left them to continue in prayer, they fell asleep again, and Peter indeed fell into temptation. Oh, he boasted at the Last Supper that he was ready to die with Jesus, but a few hours later he was slicing off an ear of the high priest's servant and then denying that he even knew Jesus. At the third denial he saw the Lord turn and look at him, and he wept bitterly.[8]

Peter who had been so close to the Master, a chosen apostle, the rock, had hit a wall in his spiritual journey. He was proud, prayerless, powerless, and pitiful. Fortunately, this is not the end of the story. Peter saw the empty tomb; he heard the Great Commission to go make disciples of all nations.[9] Jesus had specific final words for him, again inviting Peter, the rock, "Follow me" (John 21:19). And Peter did follow Jesus to witness his ascension and wait in Jerusalem for the outpouring of the promised Holy Spirit.

> Once when he was eating with them, he commanded them, "Do not leave Jerusalem until the Father sends you the gift he promised, as I told you before. John baptized with water, but in just a few days you will be baptized with the Holy Spirit" (*Acts 1:4-5*).

As the band of believers waited in the upper room, Peter took charge.[10] They prayed constantly as they followed Jesus' instructions and tarried. On the Day of Pentecost they were all filled with the Holy Spirit, but Peter was the one who emerged as the leader. Now humble, prayerful, courageous, and effective through the power of the Holy Spirit, Peter spoke to the crowds with boldness.[11] In Acts 3 the lame man was healed. To temple gazers surprised by what they saw, Peter asked, "Why stare at us as though we had made this man walk by our own power or godliness?" (Acts 3:12). He took this opportunity to address the crowd with the message of Jesus and brazenly told them, "You killed the author of life, but God raised him from the dead. And we are witnesses of this fact!" (Acts 3:15). Then Peter proclaimed, "Through faith in the name of Jesus this man was healed—and you know how crippled he was before. Faith in Jesus' name has healed him before your very eyes" (Acts 3:16). Notice the sight words and phrases that Peter used: *stare, witnesses, before your very eyes.* Peter then told the crowds to repent and turn to God so that their sins would be wiped away.[12] Before Peter and John were arrested the first time, the believers already totaled about five thousand men, in addition to the women and children.[13] Following their arrest, Peter, filled with the Holy Spirit, said to the council of rulers and elders that the crippled man was healed by the powerful name of Jesus, and confidently stated, "There is salvation in no one else!" (Acts 4:12).

This Peter who followed Jesus, denied him, wept bitterly, and waited in the upper room was now filled with the Holy Spirit and empowered to do the work Jesus called him to do when he said, "Follow me!" Peter raised Dorcas from the dead.[14] A unique vision convinced him that Gentiles also were included in God's plan.[15] People were watching.

> As a result of the apostles' work, sick people were brought out into the streets on beds and mats so that Peter's shadow might fall across some of them as he went by. Crowds came from the villages around Jerusalem, bringing their sick and those possessed by evil spirits, and they were all healed (*Acts 5:15-16*).

Peter was so intent on preaching Jesus that he did not realize others were scrutinizing his life—and still are today.

Opposition came, but Peter stood firm and saw powerful results from his ministry as he proclaimed the good news of Jesus, the Messiah, Redeemer, Healer, and coming King. By reading 1 and 2 Peter, we continue to learn from the faithful apostle, the rock, about this hope of eternal life through Jesus and the call to holy living by the power of the Spirit. He teaches how to grow in faith, pay attention to Scripture, beware of false teachers, and prepare for the Lord's return. Yes, Pentecost changed everything for Peter when he waited in the upper room following the Master's call.

I also have had an upper room Pentecost in an upstairs apartment where I waited and prayed all night.

Like Peter, I, too, have been proud, prayerless, powerless, and pitiful. I was a child when I asked Jesus to forgive my sins and enter my heart; I knew that I was "born again," using the words of Jesus to Nicodemus in John 3:3, and John 3:16 became a reality. I could say with Peter, "You are the Son of the living God." However, years later as an adult, I well remember the night I crawled out of bed aware of my selfishness, powerlessness, and need of a cleansed heart. I prayed throughout the night hours, relinquishing my desires, affections, aspirations, and will, giving God my all. As morning light dawned, I knew my old self had been crucified with Christ and my desires nailed to the cross (Galatians 5:24-25). I had a personal Pentecost—this cleansed heart made possible by the shed blood of Jesus Christ. From that sunrise to this present day, God has continued leading me on a journey that daily unfolds amazing adventures with him.[16]

I have watched God do immeasurably more than I could ask or imagine (Ephesians 3:20). Yes, I can relate to Bud and Peter, both in their defeat and in their victory through the power of the Holy Spirit.

What do you do when you hit a wall, find yourself up and down, making declarations then feeling remorseful when you fail miserably, ready to give up? With Peter as an example, follow Jesus. Surrender to his lordship. Allow him to cleanse and purify your heart. Wait for the infilling of his Holy Spirit. Keep praying, reading the Word, singing, praising God, obeying, and clinging to precious promises.

The Christian journey into victory and rest is both inward and outward. God sees our heart and does his forgiving, cleansing, and healing work in the deep hidden places when we are open and willing. This transformation affects others as they witness our changed behavior and attitudes. Some changes may be evident immediately; others take place gradually as a result of spending time with God. I have learned the value of waiting quietly to listen for his leading, which takes discipline but is essential for ultimate spiritual growth. "I wait quietly before God, for my victory comes from him" (Psalm 62:1). Once his call is heard through prayer and reading Scripture prayerfully, obedience and acceptance of his plan must follow. "Serve only the LORD your God and fear him alone. Obey his commands, listen to his voice, and cling to him" (Deuteronomy 13:4). The struggle comes when the believer chooses his or her own way rather than relinquishing control to God. "The Holy Spirit says, 'Today when you hear his voice, don't harden your hearts as Israel did when they rebelled, when they tested me in the wilderness'" (Hebrews 3:7-8). A submissive heart, open for fresh infillings of the Spirit, will enter his rest. "God's promise of entering his rest still stands, so we ought to tremble with fear that some of you might fail to experience it. For this good news—that God has prepared this rest—has been announced to us just as it was to them" (Hebrews 4:1-2).

In addition to privately spending time alone with God, finding a spiritual mentor or joining a small accountability group has life-transforming merit. Stephanie Hogan in *Living in the Overflow* writes, "In my own life, Jesus has used small accountability groups to do an incredible work, taking me deeper into himself in ways I never could have known him on my own."[17] She adds, "I've learned much from others who've walked with Jesus longer than I have. Their lives let me see a different and deeper picture of who he is. . . . Just as I've received from those older in the faith, I've also had the incredible privilege to turn to the younger women in groups and let Jesus pour his life through me into them, to share in their struggles and pain, and to bring them to Jesus as we prayed together."[18]

Stephanie, who is the director of the Francis Asbury Society's Titus Women's ministry, boldly claims, "Small-group accountability is about living in the light of the presence of Jesus—together. It's not about making spiritual comparisons or offering easy answers; accountability is helping each other live, thrive, and abide in the presence of the Father, Son, and Holy Spirit, and that is something we can't do alone."[19] Beth Coppedge, Titus Women's founder, often says, "We're in him and in each other to reach a world for Jesus!"

Observing others who have entered his rest and are living the victorious Christian life, as Stephanie Hogan and Beth Coppedge are, bolsters my faith. Watching those like Simon Peter and Bud who have faced failure and have overcome it inspires me when I am walking through confusion or disappointment. Whose life are you watching? Who may be watching you? How we respond to failure and disillusionment matters both to ourselves as well as to onlookers.

I have been watching Simon Peter and Bud. Bud has memorized more scripture than anyone I know and is so intent on encouraging others to commit the Word to memory that he is oblivious that others are looking to him and sharing his story. Like Peter, Bud surrendered to the lordship of Jesus. He moved from trying to live the Christian life in his own strength to a Spirit-controlled life, and today he continues to serve God and others with great joy knowing that it is true: "He is here! He is all around you! He is everywhere!" And he longs to invade your heart and life. Follow his call, and allow the Master's words to enlarge your vision and bring abundant joy.

- Before reading Scripture, spend a few minutes quieting your heart, listening, and asking God to reveal his truth to you as you read.
- Read prayerfully, paying close attention to messages God has for you.
- Meditate on what you have read, and record revelations in your journal.

Scripture

Acts 1-12

1 and 2 Peter

Memorize 1 Peter 1:8-9

You love him even though you have never seen him. Though you do not see him now, you trust him; and you rejoice with a glorious, inexpressible joy. The reward for trusting him will be the salvation of your souls.

Suggestion

- Memorize verse nine first.
- Rewrite these verses in the first person. Example: "I love him even though I have never seen him . . ."

_____

_____

_____

_____

- Write these verses again as a prayer: "I love you, Lord . . . "

_____

_____

_____

_____

Reflection Insights

_____

_____

_____

_____

_____

_____

_____

_____

_____

_____

_____

_____

_____

_____

_____

_____

_____

_____

_____

_____

_____

_____

REJOICE AND PROCLAIM HIS GOOD NEWS

I. WITNESS THE MIRACLE

An amazing answer to prayer
leads to the next bold request.

You will receive power when the Holy Spirit comes upon you. And you will be my witnesses, telling people about me everywhere—in Jerusalem, throughout Judea, in Samaria, and to the ends of the earth (Acts 1:8).

A few moments ago I was sitting in the hair salon for a trim, watching my gifted hairdresser, who is a miracle of divine healing, snip, chat, smile, and report God stories. Seven years ago I was sitting in a hospital waiting area with more than twenty-five concerned friends while she underwent surgery for a brain tumor that had created blindness and life-threatening issues including the risks of stroke, spinal fluid leakage, paralysis, and even death. Friends and family members wept and shouted for joy when we heard from the surgeon that the operation had been successful and that Jane could see. The entire tumor had been removed, and Jane had full vision in both eyes. The surgeon did not tell us at that time that he expected the restored vision to be temporary and limited, although he had made it clear that the tumor could return.

Jane went through weeks of therapy, rehabilitation, and follow-up visits and was left with debilitating pain. During the surgery, her forehead had been removed for a short time to get to the tumor. This left her with nerve damage and horrible headaches. The pain specialist, Dr. Kim, told her that she would have to learn to live with excruciating pain since the damage was permanent. Eventually most of her days were spent in bed trying to cushion her body with pillows to find a bearable position. This condition continued for many months regardless of what pain killers were prescribed or methods of possible relief introduced.

Jane felt compelled to try to go to a special service at her church one night. At the conclusion of the service, the speaker invited anyone who would like to have prayer for healing to come forward. Jane was the first to go. I later heard this story from the speaker, who had fallen that day, suffering a severe foot injury. After a doctor's visit, she continued to experience great pain and wondered if she would be able to go to church; however, she hobbled on crutches to the platform, delivered her sermon from a chair, and continued sitting as people came for healing prayer. All the time she was thinking it seemed ironic that she was praying for others when she needed healing herself. No words were spoken. Prayers were lifted silently, and those coming for prayer did not identify themselves or the reason they were there because the speaker believed God knew the true need and would direct her prayers. She did not know my friend Jane or her condition when Jane paused before her for prayer, nor did she know until later that Jane's pain was gone before she had returned to her seat.

The next day Jane asked Dr. Kim to begin reducing her medication, although she did not tell him the headaches were gone for fear he would credit the drugs and not prayer. Since he knew there was nothing more medically he could do for her, he agreed and began gradually reducing the powerful dosage. On her last visit, Jane sensed the Holy Spirit nudging her to tell Dr. Kim of her divine healing. He agreed that God's touch could be the only explanation.[1]

Jane had been off work a couple of years but after her healing returned to her profession as a hairdresser and continues telling her story every time a client gives her an opening. She had been on a mission trip to Africa when the blindness in one eye first occurred; today she is a missionary in her hair salon, witnessing to God's healing grace and restoring power.

Twenty-plus years before, I met Jane when my husband became her pastor. We developed a friendship and prayer partnership that continued after I moved to another state. When I returned to live in her city four years ago, we began praying together again. Each month when I go to the salon for my haircut, I learn of new ways God is using Jane's testimony and gather more prayer requests.

One day I arrived at Jane's shop shortly after a young girl had delivered a Bible for a new Christ-follower I'll call Susie. A few months before, Susie had confessed to Jane that she was addicted to gambling. A man waiting for his appointment overheard this conversation and told Jane he was going to ask his prayer group to pray for the young woman, and Jane enlisted her Bible fellowship class to pray. Several months later Susie reported exciting news. She had become a Christian, found a job, and was getting help for her addiction. This friend from her past who delivered the Bible had also recently given her heart to Jesus. That was two years ago. Today I asked Jane for an update on Susie and learned that she is still moving forward!

Even with these wonderful answers to prayer, Jane is grieving today, Valentine's Day, as she remembers the events of two months before. On Wednesday, December 14, Jane had talked with her brother Steve on the phone in the morning, worked in her salon all day, attended prayer meeting at church in the evening, then moments before crawling into bed received an unexpected phone call with bad news from her brother Ross. He urged her to drive immediately to the hospital where their forty-two-year-old brother, Steve, had been rushed by paramedics.

When Jane and her mother raced into the emergency room, they received the crushing news that Steve had been pronounced dead of a massive heart attack on arrival at the hospital. Steve's three teenage sons poured out the story, confirmed by Ross, who had been on the phone with his brother from the time the paramedics were called until they left the house with Steve in the ambulance. Ross had talked on the phone with Steve several times throughout the day regarding a work issue; Steve had not been sick at all, but about bedtime he became violently ill. Both Ross and the 911 center were called. When the emergency crew arrived at the home, they began to work on Steve, but he lost consciousness. After a few minutes of CPR, Steve rallied and began to call out to God for forgiveness and told his boys he was dying; he then fell back, continuing to cry out to God with groans of "O God, forgive me, help me," as he was carried on a stretcher to the emergency vehicle.

For several weeks beforehand, Jane had been placing Steve's name into a prayer request urn at church. God did not answer in the way she expected; however, the next Sunday she placed a card into the praise receptacle beside the prayer request container that she had visited so many weeks before. Mark Batterson says, "Part of praying hard is persisting in prayer even when we don't get the answer we want. It's choosing to believe that God has a better plan."[2]

Steve was a senior in high school when my husband came to be pastor of his family's church. He was faithful to attend church and befriended younger teens. Somewhere along the journey to young adulthood, he lost his way and stopped going to church. His family never gave up praying for him, though. Even so, perhaps they have found themselves, like Ann Voskamp after the death of her nephew, saying, "I'd write this story differently."[3]

Ann's brother-in-law responded, "Maybe you don't want to change the story, because you don't know what a different ending holds."[4] Ann confessed, "There's a reason I am not writing the story and God is. He knows how it all works out, where it all leads, what it all means."[5] She concluded that the losses that puncture our world may become holes to see through to God.[6] Jane, like Ann, has made a choice to accept those things she does not understand and to see God in the mystery of it all.

As I sat in Steve's memorial service, I watched friends from his past youth group gather; some had traveled for hours from other states. The church chapel was packed. Those who came to honor him filled the seats or stood where they could find a space and heard the song "Turn Your Eyes upon Jesus." Family and friends listened as the minister encouraged us to look to Jesus. Not only is he the babe of Christmas, but he is also the resurrected Lord, our coming King. Prior to his crucifixion, he promised that the Comforter would come and the Holy Spirit would be outpoured on believers after his death and resurrection. Before his ascension into heaven, he declared that his followers would receive power from the Holy Spirit and be his witnesses. That was not only a word for the early church in Acts but is also our calling today wherever we find ourselves. I look to Jane as an example of a present-day Christ-follower who lives her witness.

Yes, Jane daily lives out God's faithfulness in times of trial—not only in past but also in present grief. She witnesses to her family—her Jerusalem—and her clients from around the community—her Judea. She has been women's ministries director for fifty churches in her denomination in the southwest quadrant of her state—her Samaria—and for years she was missionary president of her church and made mission trips. Her miracle story in *God Sightings* has traveled far. Jane's witness has gone to the ends of the earth.

Unlike Jane, who was on a Christian mission trip to Africa when blindness in one eye developed, Saul of Tarsus (later called Paul) was on the road to Damascus with authorization to persecute Christians when he was struck with blindness.[7] This unexpected divine encounter led him to spread the good news about Jesus on three major missionary journeys. Paul is an example of how God can change the hardest of hearts and enlist them to partner with him in miracles. Paul turned from ravaging the church, dragging men and women to prison,[8] and breathing threats and murder against the disciples of the Lord[9] to establishing churches throughout what are known today as Turkey, Greece, and Italy. He preached Christ to high government officials and suffered much persecution for the sake of the Lord. Many of Paul's inspired letters written to churches that he started are found in the New Testament. Every time I read the stories of Paul's ministry and his New Testament epistles, I am witnessing miracles and reminded anew of God's mighty power to restore and bring freedom.

One of Paul's early letters was written to the believers in the region of Galatia where he traveled on his first missionary journey. In the opening chapter he wrote, "You know what I was like when I followed the Jewish religion—how I violently persecuted God's church. I did my best to destroy it. . . . But even before I was born, God chose me and called me by his marvelous grace. . . . Then it pleased him to reveal his Son to me so that I would proclaim the Good News about Jesus to the Gentiles" (Galatians 1:13-16). The subject of his message to the Galatians is the miracle of freedom in Christ, freedom from sin, freedom to love and serve—all available because of grace. He encouraged the Galatians to walk in freedom and follow the Spirit's leading in every part of their lives.[10]

Centuries after Paul wrote his letter to the Galatians, the miracle of God's grace extended through Jesus Christ is the message that my friend Jane proclaims also. She witnesses to grace and freedom in Christ as she demonstrates the fruit of the Spirit that Paul lists in Galatians 5:22-23. Anytime we see love, joy, peace, patience, kindness, goodness, faithfulness, gentleness, and self-control exemplified in a life, we are witnessing a miracle, especially when that fruit is evident in times of grief and trials! Walking by the Spirit does not exempt us from difficulties in this life. Both Paul and Jane have weathered storms on their knees and discovered that one miraculous answer to prayer leads to another bold request. Jane, a living miracle, and multitudes of believers who have studied the life of Paul and his prayers in the New Testament know how to pray hard and pray through.

"By definition, praying hard is praying when it is hard to pray. And it's the hard times that teach us to pray hard. But if you keep praying through, the peace that transcends understanding will guard your heart and your mind."[11] Keep praying hard even in hard times, and watch miracles unfold, filling your heart with praise in the midst of trials; then proclaim the good news.

Reflections

- Make a list of miracles you have witnessed.

_____

_____

_____

_____

_____

- Share one God story with someone this month.
- Make a prayer request list that would require miracles.

_____

_____

_____

_____

_____

_____

- Prayerfully choose a fruit of the Spirit that you long to see developed in yourself.

Scripture

- Reread Acts 9:1-31.
- Read Acts 13-15.
- Read Galatians 5:13-6:10 slowly each day, and pray for the Holy Spirit to guide your reading. Pause at 5:22-25, and allow Jesus to penetrate his message into your heart so that you will be prepared to be his witness everywhere he leads you, thus reaping a harvest of blessings.

Memorize Galatians 5:22-25

The Holy Spirit produces this kind of fruit in our lives: love, joy, peace, patience, kindness, goodness, faithfulness, gentleness, and self-control. There is no law against these things! Those who belong to Christ Jesus have nailed the passions and desires of their sinful nature to his cross and crucified them there. Since we are living by the Spirit, let us follow the Spirit's leading in every part of our lives.

Suggestion

Find a partner to work with in memorizing. You may choose to memorize only Galatians 5:22-23; however, read verses 24-25 often, and they will become embedded in your heart and mind.

Reflection Insights

11. TELL YOUR STORY

What you have seen and heard may touch another heart.

Then Jesus called for the children and said to the disciples, "Let the children come to me. Don't stop them! For the Kingdom of God belongs to those who are like these children. I tell you the truth, anyone who doesn't receive the Kingdom of God like a child will never enter it" (Luke 18:16-17).

This morning, February 15, our daughter, Lanissa, called to tell us that our grandson Caleb had asked Jesus into his heart last night, a week before his sixth birthday. She said his eyes glowed, and with a huge smile he exclaimed that he could hardly wait to tell his car pool buddies. He proudly shared his story first thing as they climbed into the car this morning, and he also said he planned to tell his kindergarten teacher when he got to school. Both his teacher and the school nurse tearfully told Lanissa that all day Caleb enthusiastically talked about Jesus to students and adults. The little evangelist is already sharing the good news of the gospel. Jesus longs to be invited into open hearts, including those of little children.

Jesus loved children. He healed them, raised them from the dead, blessed them, and used them as examples when he taught his disciples and the multitudes. His Spirit has awakened little Caleb, and he will continue his work in this young child of his.

I can pray with the assurance that it is God's will for the fruit of the Spirit to grow in Caleb. He already has a tender heart, and I am confident that fruit increasingly will be evident in Caleb's life as he allows the spirit of Jesus to control his decisions.

Jesus on many occasions demonstrated his tender compassion; however, when faced with sin, evil forces, and temptation, he was emphatic. This is evident in his teaching when his disciples asked, "Who is greatest in the Kingdom of Heaven?" (Matthew 18:1):

> Jesus called a little child to him and put the child among them. Then he said, "I tell you the truth, unless you turn from your sins and become like little children, you will never get into the Kingdom of Heaven. So anyone who becomes as humble as this little child is the greatest in the Kingdom of Heaven. And anyone who welcomes a little child like this on my behalf is welcoming me. But if you cause one of these little ones who trusts in me to fall into sin, it would be better for you to have a large millstone tied around your neck and be drowned in the depths of the sea" (*Matthew 18:2-6*).

I am studying the teachings of Jesus and stories in the Bible to give me insight on how to guide and pray for tenderhearted Caleb.

Our family has always prayed that Caleb would live up to his name, and by nature he has traits of the Caleb of the Old Testament—courage, excitement, a positive outlook, and the ability to see things others miss. He has a keen imagination and visual acuity. He describes in great detail the mansion he plans to build someday and designs amazing structures with his building blocks, Legos, and Lincoln Logs. He is observant and surprises me as he points out things he sees that I haven't noticed. Caleb will spend hours in the backyard play area, where he loves to swing, slide, climb, and make sand villages.

One day when we had stopped playing and were sitting in the loft of the fort, I saw that faraway look in his eyes and knew he was watching something at a distance. Trying to follow his gaze, I inquired about what he was seeing. Among other things, he asked if I could see the water tower. I squinted and could barely see the tip on the horizon miles away. I pray that Caleb will also develop keen spiritual vision and will point others in the right direction as he shares his story of faith with courage.

I have two Bible characters that I use as examples when I pray for Caleb, one in the Old Testament and one in the New Testament. In Numbers 13, I look at the characteristics of the Israelite Caleb when he reported to Moses and the multitude wandering in the wilderness about his exploration into Canaan. He saw a land of plenty flowing with milk, honey, and luscious fruit and believed God would help them conquer the territory in spite of the giants. He was bold, had faith, and spoke up for what was God's will in spite of opposition and the resistance of ten of the other twelve explorers. "But Caleb tried to quiet the people as they stood before Moses. 'Let's go at once to take the land,' he said. 'We can certainly conquer it'" (Numbers 13:30). The Lord honored Caleb's faith and obedience when he said, "But my servant Caleb has a different attitude than the others have. He has remained loyal to me, so I will bring him into the land he explored. His descendants will possess their full share of that land" (Numbers 14:24). My desire is that my grandson Caleb will also develop into a man of character and strong leadership seeing the possibilities with God on his side, and like one of Marissa's favorite sayings "will stand for right even if he finds himself standing alone."

Timothy is the New Testament believer I have chosen to think of when praying for Caleb. Paul invited Timothy, who was well respected in the lower Galatia area, to join him on his second missionary jour-ney.[1] Paul mentored Timothy. Sometimes they traveled together; on other occasions Paul sent Timothy elsewhere to encourage the church-es. Later in his ministry Paul wrote letters to Timothy warning, "Don't let anyone think less of you because you are young. Be an example to all believers in what you say, in the way you live, in your love, your faith, and your purity" (1 Timothy 4:12). I pray that verse often for Caleb, that he will not let anyone steal his joy while he is young and that he will be an example in word, deed, love, faith, and purity.

These Bible stories and many others have inspired me! As I read Scripture, I visualize myself and others being involved in God's story of redemption. Both Caleb's story in the Bible and little Caleb's recent testimony have deeply touched me. Paul, investing in the life of young Timothy, encourages me to walk alongside the youth of my world—teaching, training, loving.

A story told to me by my friend Rhonda has impacted me and en-couraged me to pray fervently for what seems like the hardest teenage heart. Anna, in Rhonda's teen Bible study group, invited Nan, her high school classmate, to attend church with her.[2] Nan began to taunt Anna in front of her peers, calling her a church girl and making fun of her because of her faith. Anna shared this with her youth pastor's wife, Rhonda, and they began to pray for Nan. Eventually Nan, who claimed to be an atheist, came to church, went to youth camp in the summer, and with Rhonda and her husband leading her, gave her heart to Jesus the last day before boarding the bus home.

Nan had been involved in very destructive behaviors and knew she would have to make drastic changes. That evening she sat up most of the night sharing about her new faith with her single-parent mom. The next day she told her best friend and discovered that the friend had gone to another Christian camp and had asked Jesus into her heart.

Nan knew she needed to tell two other girls in their group that she would no longer be involved in some of their previous harmful activities. To her amazement they said, "We've wanted out of those habits but didn't know how to tell you." That's when Nan, with mentoring from Rhonda, decided to start a Bible study with these friends, sharing stories from Scripture!

Stories from the life of Jesus can speak truth into difficult situations. Hal Perkins has written a book titled *If Jesus Were a Parent*. Hal's son, David, leads prayer gatherings for thousands of college students. When David was in seventh grade, his dad noticed that his son no longer met him at the door at the end of his work day. One afternoon when he went looking for David, he found him crumpled up in his bed. His dad wrote, "This was uncharacteristic of my happy, outgoing junior high son. . . . The pain in his countenance told me he was not okay."[3] As his sad story unfolded, David's dad learned that his small-framed son was being verbally and physically abused by his peers at his new school. He had gone from being one of the most popular kids at his previous school to being mocked and mistreated daily.

As Perkins tells this touching story in his book, he explains how he listened and prayed with David and spoke truth from God's Word into his situation. Eventually David led the ring leader, Joe, to Jesus; they started an early-morning prayer meeting at school, which began with five and grew to sixty; fifteen years later, fifty to eighty students were still meeting every morning to study the Bible and pray before school.[4] Many became Christ-followers—several are pastors and missionaries, Joe became a missionary trainer, and Dave directs a university prayer and disciple-making ministry.[5] A mentoring parent and a supporting teacher helped David overcome with amazing results, and his story continues as he touches the lives of thousands through his ministry to young adults today.

God also uses neighbors and children's workers to speak truth into the lives of young hearts. A man in my granddaughter Marissa's church has been a mentor to children for years. I asked Marissa to interview Mr. Loyd, and she responded, "I bet that can be arranged. I like Mr. Loyd. He's friendly. He was my prayer partner one year." Here is the story Marissa uncovered:

Loyd Olsan's journey with kids started while he was in the Air Force and continued forty-plus years in many churches and community organizations throughout his travels. When Loyd and his wife, Naomi, moved to Tulsa, Oklahoma, in 2002, they gave away all their children's ministry materials because they were both battling major health issues. Loyd had just finished sixteen months of cancer treatment, and several weeks in intensive care had taken its toll on Naomi. However, he said, "Tulsa was the most unusual door that the Lord opened!"

He wrote this part of his story for Marissa:

One morning in September 2002, I was sitting at our breakfast nook and heard a lot of voices outside. Much to my surprise, there were about fifteen kids in my front yard waiting to catch a school bus at 7:00 A.M. and another large group that caught a bus at 8:10 A.M. The next morning I went out to investigate. Children are so innocent. When I asked them what was going on, one of them volunteered, "Oh, we used to catch the bus down the street, but they ran us off." I was stunned for a moment and then replied, "Well, I'm glad they did, because my wife and I love children."

That was the beginning; every morning I was out with the children. We played games until the bus came. In bad weather, I let them come into the garage. Several moms started coming, and we became friends. My wife and I decided that the Lord had opened an unexpected door, and we started a Good News Club in our home every Thursday afternoon. In March 2007, the Lord took my Naomi home despite the care of the most loving medical doctors, which included Marissa's dad. I continued having the Bible club another year with the help of ladies from church and Child Evangelism Fellowship. When will the Lord open the next door? I'm not sure, but I'm willing to enter when he presents it. Life is indeed an exciting adventure when we walk with the Lord!

I finally met Loyd Olsan a few months ago. He's still active as the property manager of his church—unlocking and locking doors, turning lights on and off, and speaking a word of encouragement to everyone he greets, especially the children and their parents. I want to follow Loyd's example, watching for God to open avenues to invest in children, teens, and young adults. His story inspires me!

Who are the children God is calling you to lead to Jesus and disciple? Be on watch—the fields are ripe for harvest.[6] Does he have a Timothy for you to mentor? Is there some young person who would benefit from hearing your story? Keep alert! Perhaps he has a lesson to teach you from a child who is excited about his or her faith and wants everyone to have the joy of knowing Jesus. Those are thoughts I'm pondering and questions I'm asking myself as I meditate on the teachings of Jesus regarding children and being childlike in faith.

My prayer: *O Father, Lord of heaven and earth, help me to see through your eyes. Send more mentors like Loyd, Naomi, and Rhonda for today's youth! Empower parents who know you to lead their children in paths of righteousness for your name's sake, like David's dad, Hal, and Caleb's mom, Lanissa. We long for more men like Paul, Timothy, and Caleb of old who continue to mentor through the ages as we read their stories in your Word. I give you thanks for young adults who love you and are making a difference in their world, like David, Nan, and Anna, and for children like little Caleb, who has opened his heart to you and joyfully tells his story, spreading your good news. What I have seen and heard from the stories of these young disciples and their mentors has touched my heart and has inspired me to continue to tell my story.*

Reflections

- Intentionally make a difference in the life of a child each day for the remainder of this month.
- Choose one child a day for focused prayer, and ask God if there is a child you can lead to Christ by telling your story.

Scripture

- Acts 16:1-5
- 2 Timothy
- Read 2 Timothy 3:16-17 daily this week.

Memorize 1 Timothy 4:12 (NIV)

Don't let anyone look down on you because you are young, but set an example for the believers in speech, in life, in love, in faith, and in purity.

Suggestion

- Make a list: speech, life, love, faith, purity.
- Memorize the list first.
- Focus on one characteristic in the list each day.
- If you are no longer young, you may want to change the word to another term that identifies you.

Reflection Insights

PRAISE AND CELEBRATE WITH OTHERS

I. OPEN YOUR HEART AND HOME

United prayer can change the world!

On the Sabbath we went a little way outside the city to a riverbank, where we thought people would be meeting for prayer, and we sat down to speak with some women who had gathered there. One of them was Lydia from Thyatira, a merchant of expensive purple cloth, who worshiped God. As she listened to us, the Lord opened her heart, and she accepted what Paul was saying. She was baptized along with other members of her household, and she asked us to be her guests. "If you agree that I am a true believer in the Lord," she said, "come and stay at my home." And she urged us until we agreed (Acts 16:13-15).

After Paul saw a vision of a man pleading with him to come to Macedonia and help them, he and Silas traveled to the Macedonian city of Philippi. On the Sabbath when they went to the riverbank to find a place of prayer, they discovered a group of women gathered there. Lydia, a businesswoman, was the only one named. She opened the door of her heart to the message of Jesus and opened the door of her home to Paul and Silas as well.

One day as they were going to the place of prayer, a demon-possessed girl began following them, shouting, "These men are servants of the Most High God, and they have come to tell you how to be saved" (Acts 16:17). Since she earned a lot of money as a fortune teller for her masters, they were angry when Paul commanded the demon to come out of her in the name of Jesus Christ. Their hopes of earning money at her expense now shattered, they caused an uproar, which landed Paul and Silas in prison after a severe beating.

"Around midnight Paul and Silas were praying and singing hymns to God, and the other prisoners were listening. Suddenly, there was a massive earthquake, and the prison was shaken to its foundations. All the doors immediately flew open, and the chains of every prisoner fell off!" (Acts 16:25-26). The frightened jailer asked, "Sirs, what must I do to be saved?" (Acts 16:30), and Paul held a midnight baptismal service before being released and returning to Lydia's home where he encouraged the believers once again before leaving town. From there the gospel spread throughout Europe, and the course of history was changed. Combine praying, praising, and singing hymns, and you are sure to see unusual doors open. This is so even today, many years removed from that prison midnight worship service in Philippi or the riverbank prayer meeting with Lydia and friends.

For centuries women from many nations have been praying in small groups inspired by Lydia from Philippi. I first learned of the Lydia Prayer Movement in September 2005 when I was given a brochure promoting a women's conference to be held the following fall. On the back of the folder was a brief announcement about Lydia prayer groups being formed in various locations. I was intrigued and learned that

Beth Kinlaw Coppedge, the founder of Titus Women's Ministry, was the visionary for these prayer gatherings.

Although I had never met Beth, I made an appointment with her and traveled to her home to learn more. As she shared passionately about forming small prayer groups around the world inspired by the story of Lydia, she turned to me and asked, "What do you think?" This was the beginning of my journey with the Lydia Prayer Ministry, which now includes scores of small prayer groups in many countries praying in homes, churches, workplaces, drive-in eateries, riverbanks, and other creative locations. These women are praying for revival and for God's glory to be revealed, not only in our own homes, churches, and communities but in all the nations of the world as well.

The vision of women praying in small groups around the globe came to Beth and a prayer partner a few months before as they knelt beside her blue couch and poured out their hearts to Jesus. He brought them to Acts 1:8, and they concluded,

> The commandment was to share Jesus with an ever-broadening audience, starting with their immediate surroundings and eventually reaching the whole world. In this they believed Jesus was also giving them a pattern for prayer: beginning with prayer for their inner circles of family and friends, then widening to their communities, their country, and the world. They were in such awe and wonder of what Jesus showed them that they could only be still as the sweetness of His presence filled their hearts.[1]

In less than an hour after opening the door of her home and sharing her vision, Beth had invited me to be the Lydia Prayer coordinator and suggested that perhaps I was to be the prayer chaplain for the women's conference being planned for the following October. From that meeting, Beth's vision of women opening their homes for small prayer groups also became mine, and I drove away from her home asking God if he was opening this door, inviting me to join him in another adventure.

Soon Lydia prayer guides, men's prayer guides, leader's packets, and other materials were published. I enlisted a large group of prayer partners, and Lydia prayer clusters began to form around the world as well as Psalm One men's prayer teams and little Daniel and Lydia groups. Miracle stories immediately surfaced as a result of this massive prayer network. Beth Coppedge often says, "Give Jesus your kitchen table and coffee mugs, and let him use them to bring revival to the people around you." Amazingly, Jesus uses a few gathered by a riverside, kneeling beside a couch, or sitting at a kitchen table to bring about his redemptive plan.[2]

I discovered the power of united prayer many years before I met Beth. My first small prayer circle was in Kansas City with a few wives of seminarians who met in the home of a professor's wife. From Missouri God led my husband to become pastor of a church in New Jersey, a state we had never visited. We knew no one in the church or even in the state when we drove our U-Haul truck of belongings from a three-room furnished apartment to a four-bedroom parsonage just across the Pennsylvania state line near Philadelphia. It was truly a venture of faith.

A few months later, Curtis attended a conference on personal evangelism. He returned full of enthusiasm and offered to watch our newborn son on Tuesday mornings if I would lead a ladies' prayer group and teach them to share their faith. I indicated that I would think and pray about it; already my mind was swirling with thoughts of what I would do with such a group. I began to think of books that I could read about friendship evangelism, because up to that point the only times I had tried to share my faith I had choked up and become tearful while attempting to lead someone to Christ. I had settled for inviting others to church, hoping the pastor could tell them how to find Jesus. That was the extent of my ability to teach personal evangelism.

Much to my surprise, the next Sunday Curtis made the announcement that I would be leading a prayer group the following Tuesday morning, and there was no turning back. I recalled the things Gertrude Taylor had taught me about prayer by her example, and my dozen praying ladies saw miracles unfold. When the men evidenced God working as a response to prayer, they decided to meet one night a week at the church altar and again early Sunday morning. We were in awe as God led us into avenues of ministry; we watched our church quadruple within a few years. We not only prayed but also went to places God led us, and he did the work of transforming people of all ages from a variety of lifestyles and cultures.

One hot Sunday night in a packed auditorium with no air conditioning, Curtis ended his sermon early and was dismissing the crowd when a young man visiting for the first time stood in the midst of the congregation and said, "I came to church tonight to get saved." His wife had visited our church with her sister-in-law a few Sundays before and received Jesus as her Lord and Savior. Now he hungered to give his heart to Jesus so much that a crowded, unairconditioned auditorium was not going to deter him. That is one of multiple God stories from our praying church.

Not only were new people finding living hope, but God was also opening unexpected doors for long-time believers and leaders—including me. I attended an evangelism conference, learned of others who were using their home for friendship evangelism, and opened my door for a faith-sharing brunch. Twenty ladies came; two prayed to receive Jesus into their hearts, one an Islamic woman. This was the first of several evangelism gatherings in my home. Others in my prayer group opened their homes for faith-sharing events. In addition to neighborhood evangelism teas, we swung our doors open for fellowship meals, class socials, church singspirations, teen functions, missions planning, and every home gathering included prayer. I have learned that when we open our door for Jesus, he enters!

Last year I returned to New Jersey for a Lydia Prayer Retreat in a town a couple of hours from our previous church. Five ladies from that church drove to the prayer retreat—one eighty-year-old who was part of my first prayer group and two who were faithful teens in the church back then. Both of their mothers were in my ladies' prayer group, and these teens, now adults, are still active in ministry in the church. My heart is grateful that God has allowed me to see his mighty power continuing the good work he began years before.

Paul wrote a letter to the Philippian believers a decade after he met Lydia and her small group on the riverbank. He told them that he was certain that God who began the good work in them would continue his work "until it is finally finished on the day when Christ Jesus returns" (Philippians 1:6). That's worth rejoicing over!

Like Paul, walk through the doors God swings open for you to work alongside him. Follow Lydia's example—open the door of your home to welcome guests for Christian fellowship, and invite others to join you in prayer. United prayer can change the world one person or household at a time!

Reflections

- Find a partner to pray with each week this month, perhaps opening your home for this prayer time.
- Use scripture in Philippians to guide your prayers.

Scripture

- Acts 16
- Philippians 1-4

Memorize Philippians 4:6-7

Don't worry about anything; instead, pray about everything. Tell God what you need, and thank him for all he has done. Then you will experience God's peace, which exceeds anything we can understand. His peace will guard your hearts and minds as you live in Christ Jesus.

Suggestion

Try singing Philippians 4:6 to the tune of the verse of the song "To God Be the Glory." You will be able to sing Philippians 4:6 twice before you get to the chorus; then sing the chorus. Make up your own melody or a chant for the following verse.

Reflection Insights

II. SING FOR JOY

A song will extend hope and infuse courage.

Rejoice in the Lord always. I will say it again: Rejoice!
(Philippians 4:4, NIV).

Paul and Silas saw the doors in the Philippian jail swing open as they prayed and sang hymns at midnight. I wonder what they were singing. Could it have been Psalm 100?

Shout for joy to the LORD, all the earth. Worship the LORD with gladness; come before him with joyful songs. Know that the LORD is God. It is he who made us, and we are his; we are his people, the sheep of his pasture. Enter his gates with thanksgiving and his courts with praise; give thanks to him and praise his name. For the LORD is good and his love endures forever; his faithfulness continues through all generations (Psalm 100, NIV).

My last teaching assignment was in a Christian school. I would teach my students to sing scriptures we were learning. Psalm 100 was one of their favorites. If we were in a tense situation learning a new math concept or finishing a timed standardized test, I might abruptly begin singing, "Shout for joy." Immediately they chimed in at the top of their voices to finish the Psalm, releasing tension. Singing Scripture works wonders!

Many of the Psalms begin with praise: "I will praise the LORD at all times" (Psalm 34:1). "Let all that I am praise the LORD" (146:1). "How good to sing praises to our God!" (147:1). "Sing to the LORD a new song" (149:1). I'm imagining the Philippian jailer's family singing a new song of praise following their baptismal, for the Scripture reports, "His entire household rejoiced because they all believed in God" (Acts 16:34).

The miracle of the jailer's salvation and ours is made possible by Jesus, the Lamb of God, who sang a hymn with his disciples on their last night together before he went to Gethsemane to pray. "Then they sang a hymn and went out to the Mount of Olives" (Matthew 26:30; Mark 14:26). Throughout the Bible, this combination of singing and prayer precedes miracles and victories.

Paul's formula: prayer + singing praises = miracles.

Paul's model prayer for the Philippians includes thanks, requests made with joy, and confidence that God will continue his good work.[1] Within his letter he names his desires that they will—

- overflow with love and grow in knowledge and understanding;
- live pure and blameless lives, leaving the past behind;
- be filled with the fruit of salvation—the righteous character produced by Jesus Christ;
- agree wholeheartedly, working together for one purpose;
- shine brightly for Christ with his humble attitude;
- rejoice, be considerate, experience peace, press ahead;
- do everything without complaining and arguing;
- hold firmly to the word of life; and
- bring glory and praise to God.

I delight to pray for myself and others with my Bible open to Paul's list. I sometimes send scripture prayers and songs by e-mail to encourage loved ones. Paul did not have the luxury of today's technology—computers, Internet, e-mail, smartphones, or overnight delivery—yet even in prison he found a way to communicate grace, encouragement, and instruction to the churches he started on his missionary journeys. I'm guessing that he had no idea how far-reaching his singing, prayers, and messages would go or how long his letters would be circulated.

Neither do you or I. This week I have communicated with prayer partners in Vanuatu, Madagascar, Germany, and other nations in at least four continents. Friends pray for my ministry and the readers of my books in all those countries, as well as in Kenya, Hungary, China, and nations I must search the globe to find. I also have prayer team members scattered throughout the United States who are natives of India, Argentina, Mexico, Guatemala, British Guyana, Vietnam, Singapore—the list is too long to enumerate—and they in turn invite their friends worldwide to join them in prayer. As a result, God has taken the books he commissioned me to write to people I will never meet and places to which I will never travel. This amazes me, puts a song in my heart, and makes me want to shout for joy!

I imagine Paul would be singing and shouting for joy today if he knew we were reading his epistles. When Paul acknowledged in his letter to the Philippian believers that all that happened to him had helped spread the good news, you hear only rejoicing. In fact, he uses the words "happy," "joy," and "rejoice" more than a dozen times in this short book.

When Marissa was two and a half, she stayed with us a week while her parents moved. I helped her memorize Philippians 4:4 to surprise her parents when we took her to her new home. She would say, "Rejoice in the Lord always. I will say it again, rejoice—Philippians 4:4" (NIV). Then we would sing it. A few months after I taught Marissa that verse, my fourth graders memorized Philippians 4:4-8. Each week we would memorize another verse, and I would teach them a melody to aid in memorization and retention. I believe God delights to hear us sing his Word.

Tomorrow I will be flying to a songwriters' retreat in Tennessee. The "Come to the Fire" worship team will be writing songs and recording them for the next conference. We are praying that God will give us the songs that are on his heart, the ones he wants to hear us sing. A few days before the songwriters' retreat last March, I had been reading an Old Testament story of the Israelite army marching into battle with the trumpets and musicians leading the way as God had instructed them. I sensed God speaking a message to me and wrote, "Enter the battle praising me. Fight the battle praising me. Emerge from the battle praising me." That picture became the opening lyrics to the song "The Great I Am," which has carried one of my Lydia sisters through a dark season in her life. Amazingly, she was the one he inspired to write the song before she knew that it would become her battle cry and miracle weapon! Singing his praises is a powerful way to pray. Paul, in the dungeon, knew that!

We enter the battle praising You, Lord of Heaven's Army.
We fight the battle praising You, Lord of Heaven's Army.
The great I Am! The great I Am! The great I Am!
Jesus, You're the Prince of Peace,
    King of kings, Almighty God
Alpha, Omega, the beginning and end
Messiah, You're the Living God, Emmanuel, Ancient of Days
Savior, Redeemer, who is the Lamb
Jesus! Word of God!
Jesus! Cornerstone!
Jesus! Conqueror! We lift You up!
The great I Am! The great I Am! The great I Am![2]

The armies of heaven lifted praise the night of our Savior's birth: "Suddenly the angel was joined by a vast host of others—the armies of

heaven—praising God and saying, 'Glory to God in highest heaven'"
(Luke 2:13-14).

Join the hosts of heaven; sing for joy to the great I Am! Follow him
rejoicing and watching for miracles to unfold. Praise and celebrate with
others. Perhaps God wants to use you and your prayer partners, as he
did Paul and his partners, to change the world! It will be surprising to
see how far reaching God will take your united prayers and praise to
extend grace and infuse courage.

Reflections

- For the remainder of the month, sing your prayers daily. Shout
  for joy, and make a joyful noise unto the Lord.
- Use a hymnal and recordings of Christian music to guide your
  prayers.
- Make up your own melodies or chants to scripture.
- Offer a prayer of encouragement for and extend grace to someone far away.

Scripture

Reread Philippians, pausing often to meditate and pray.

Memorize

Choose a scripture from Philippians to memorize.

Suggestion

Review boosts retention. Review previous verses you have memorized.

Reflection Insights

LAUGH AND PREPARE FOR THE ADVENTURE

1. LIVE WITH EXPECTANCY

A message can lighten and enrich your journey.

And now, dear brothers and sisters, we want you to know what will happen to the believers who have died so you will not grieve like people who have no hope. For since we believe that Jesus died and was raised to life again, we also believe that when Jesus returns, God will bring back with him the believers who have died (1 Thessalonians 4:13-14).

After Paul left Philippi, he traveled to Thessalonica and for three Sabbaths went to the Jewish synagogue, where he explained the messianic prophecies and proclaimed that Jesus was indeed the promised Messiah. Although Paul was in Thessalonica only a few weeks before the persecution became so intense that he journeyed south to Berea, he left behind enough believers that a church was established. We know this because a few years later he wrote them a letter commending their loving deeds and enduring hope. He was grateful that they had received the message he had delivered with joy from the Holy Spirit in spite of the severe suffering it brought them.[1] He praised them, saying they had become an example to all the believers in Greece. *And now the word of the Lord is ringing out from you to people everywhere, even beyond Macedonia and Achaia, for wherever we go we find people telling us about your faith in God* (1 Thessalonians 1:8).

It seems it couldn't get any better than this, but it does. *And they speak of how you are looking forward to the coming of God's Son from heaven—Jesus, whom God raised from the dead* (1 Thessalonians 1:10).

Believers in Jesus the Messiah continue to look forward to his return as they journey onward by faith, proclaiming his good news no matter what circumstances they encounter along the way.

The day before we were to leave with our daughter's family for a Thanksgiving vacation to Gulf Shores and Fort Morgan, Alabama, we heard a sermon at their church on the subject of Christ's return and the resurrection of the dead. The pastor asked the audience if we had experienced an "It doesn't get any better than this!" moment, then gave a personal example. He followed his story with the announcement that even in our "It doesn't get any better than this" times on earth, for Christ's followers it *does* get better. Then he launched into his message on the second coming in his series of sermons on life after death and heaven, which he called the "After Party."

The next day our daughter's family of five, plus Curtis and I, loaded into Lanissa's SUV. Her husband, Clay, was the driver, and Lanissa was beside him on the passenger side. PePa Curtis and two-year-old Laney were in the middle two seats, with Caleb, Calvin, and me filling the back row—MiMi (me) wedged between two grandsons. We had been warned to pack lightly, but seven people going to the beach for a week have to take their stuff, and every square inch of the vehicle was stuffed as we embarked our thirteen-hour adventure!

Within a few miles, fourth-grader Calvin asked to play the "Would You Rather" game. Everyone participated, laughing and commenting about each answer. With a big grin on my face, I exclaimed, "It doesn't get any better than this!" Since Calvin had been in "big" church with us the day before, he caught it!

The second day we made a quick stop at a market for Lanissa to buy supplies for the beach house. I stayed in the car with the children while Clay and Curtis went to the convenience store next door to get snacks. Laney was excited when her dad returned with a bottle of green "Bug Juice" drink for her. Since it had a sports tab lid, he thought it would be safe from spills.

We were engaged in conversation as we drove the few miles back to the beach house unaware that Laney had discovered that when turned upside down, she could watch the green drops fall from the bottle into her lap. She was quietly entertained until she handed the empty bottle to her mom. Lanissa shouted, "Who bought Laney Bug Juice? It's all over her and my car!"

Get the picture: Calvin, Caleb, and I are watching from the back row. The guilty driver with PePa sitting beside him in the passenger seat are both looking straight ahead with PePa relieved that he isn't the one in trouble this time—but Lanissa doesn't know that. Laney is behind her dad sitting in a pool of green liquid holding the empty bottle, and mom beside her is continuing her highly emotional "My car is ruined!" outburst. Calvin leaned forward and said, "Mom! Remember—we're on vacation!"

I burst into uncontrollable laughter when he leaned back with a sigh and said, "It doesn't get any better than this!" Then he whispered to me, "Did you catch the sarcasm?" That wasn't the last time on our vacation that we heard those words, laughed, and enjoyed the adventure.

Retelling this revives fond memories, and I have many treasured memories of spiritual blessings when I thought it couldn't get any better only to discover later that God has new truth to reveal and added blessings, giving me another occasion to say, "It really can't get any better than this!" I'm confident he will continue to expand my joyful journey heavenward, but the memories of past spiritual peaks bring smiles as I look forward to new vistas.

After Paul encouraged the Thessalonian believers in chapter one, he wrote of fond memories: *Therefore, we never stop thanking God that when you received his message from us. . . . You accepted what we said as the very word of God—which, of course, it is. And this word continues to work in you who believe* (1 Thessalonians 2:13).

Could it possibly get any better than this? Yes, it does: *After all, what gives us hope and joy, and what will be our proud reward and crown as we stand before our Lord Jesus when he returns? It is you! Yes, you are our pride and joy* (1 Thessalonians 2:19-20).

Then in chapter three Paul is rejoicing about the "It doesn't get any better than this" report Timothy brought when Paul was unable to travel back to Thessalonica:

It gives us new life to know that you are standing firm in the Lord (1 Thessalonians 3:8).

But what Paul says next proves that he knows it *can* get better, because he prays, *May God our Father and our Lord Jesus bring us to you very soon. And may the Lord make your love for one another and for all people grow and overflow, just as our love for you overflows. May he, as a result, make your hearts strong, blameless, and holy as you stand before God our Father when our Lord Jesus comes again with all his holy people. Amen* (1 Thessalonians 3:11-13).

These "better than this" passages speak of joy in serving Jesus while looking forward to his return. In chapter four Paul advises the young church to live to please God as he points them to the hope of the resurrection and explains that the dead in Christ will rise from their graves; then the living Christians will join them. *Then, together with them, we who are still alive and remain on the earth will be caught up in the clouds to meet the Lord in the air. Then we will be with the Lord forever* (1 Thessalonians 4:17).

In chapter five Paul reminds his readers: *Christ died for us so that, whether we are dead or alive when he returns, we can live with him forever* (1 Thessalonians 5:10).

Paul is teaching what Jesus proclaimed—that everyone who believes in the Son of Man will have eternal life.[2] One of the first Bible verses that Calvin memorized contained the words of Jesus to Nicodemus: *For God so loved the world that he gave his one and only Son, that whoever believes in him shall not perish but have eternal life* (John 3:16, NIV).

A couple of weeks ago Calvin told me that although he asked Jesus into his heart when he was three, he had recently asked him in again—just to make sure. When I think of Calvin's future as a Christ-follower, I wonder what battles he may encounter, especially after reading persecution stories from Paul's ministry. My thoughts turn to joy when I am reminded that eternal life begins here on earth when we receive Jesus as our Savior; however, as long as we are in this world, though heaven-bound, we will have troubles. Calvin already knows about facing trials, both minor and major. When he was younger, his happy world could fall apart in a moment if things didn't seem to be going right, and I would try to help him recover from his "bad day" gloom by making him smile or encouraging him to look for the good in what seemed like a bad situation.

Paul's very bad day in the Philippian dungeon turned into a midnight jubilee because he knew how to find treasures in darkness by allowing the light of the Son to penetrate. To lighten your journey on dark days, watch for nuggets of hope and sacred riches that may be hidden there.

And I will give you treasures hidden in the darkness—secret riches. I will do this so you may know that I am the LORD, the God of Israel, the one who calls you by name (Isaiah 45:3).

My prayer is that Calvin will learn to search for treasures in troubled times. He's already had his share of trials for a ten-year-old. His first traumatic hospital experience came when he was a few weeks old. At age five, he was in and out of the hospital nine times within a couple of months. His disease was not the only battle Calvin was facing at that time. His family was moving to another state, and he was grief stricken to be leaving his loyal friends and gifted teachers.

Other great sadnesses were bombarding the family. His baby brother had serious issues surrounding his birth and also suffered physical problems. A few months later his mom endured several hospitalizations, and recently the mother of one of his school friends died. Yes, in this world Calvin will have hardships, but he has the hope of eternal life in heaven.

We had hundreds of friends praying for Calvin and his family during his illness, and he recovered. Sometimes he wants to show me the photo album his mother prepared of that traumatic preschool year. He talks about those days freely because the beautiful scrapbook is filled with happy memories interlaced with the trials. I have no idea what future battles Calvin will face, but he has already seen the value of prayer and many "It doesn't get any better than this" moments in the midst of hard times.

When Calvin's life was in chaos at age five, Lanissa prayed that he would always know to take his fears and hurts to Jesus. That's what he did today when he faced trauma due to tornadoes in the area. On the way home from school, he and his brother had to take cover in the pantry of a friend's home. When Lanissa asked Calvin and Caleb what they did in the pantry with several friends, they said, "We huddled under a blanket and prayed that no one would die."

Paul is a wonderful role model for Calvin in times of fear and danger. The great missionary evangelist faced frequent frightening times, including storms at sea, shipwreck,[3] tribulation, and persecution, but he knew how to pray in all circumstances, remain courageous in the face of disaster, and spread joyful hope throughout his missionary journeys. Perhaps the trials Calvin is facing as a child are strengthening him for what may be ahead.

Paul's final advice to the young Thessalonian church on how to live while awaiting Christ's return is good for a young believer like Calvin in today's world:

- Show respect to your leaders in the Lord's work.
- Live peacefully; warn those who are lazy.
- Be patient with all; don't pay back evil with evil.
- Try to do good to each other; never stop praying.
- Be thankful in all circumstances; always be joyful.

Paul both enlightens and lightens the earthly journey for the Thessalonians and for readers of his letters today. He lightens the load with commendations, prayers, blessings, love, pleasant memories, joyful reminders, and assurance of Christ's return. He enlightens us to the hope of the resurrection but cautions us to keep working because Christ will return unexpectedly—no one knows when. He makes it clear that God's will is for his people to live holy lives and share in his kingdom.[4] Paul prays for the Thessalonians, that the God of peace will sanctify them through and through,[5] and reminds them that even though they are Kingdom people,[6] children of light,[7] they must be on guard, stay alert,[8] and hold on to what is good.[9]

Paul's final greeting in 1 Thessalonians is my prayer today for Calvin and the readers of *Simply Rejoicing*:

Now may the God of peace make you holy in every way, and may your whole spirit and soul and body be kept blameless until our Lord Jesus Christ comes again. God will make this happen, for he who calls you is faithful (1 Thessalonians 5:23-24).

It doesn't get any better than this on earth as we wait with expectancy for Christ's return. May Paul's message to the Thessalonians both lighten and enlighten your journey heavenward. Mark Buchanan says, "God intends the holy life be an odyssey of wonder."[10] God gives us heavenly moments here on earth so that we may have a glimpse of what is to come.

"During the closing days of the Second World War, a hospital in Nuremberg, Germany, was damaged by extensive bombing. After cleaning up the rubble, someone painted on the wall of one of the wards, as translated—'We don't know what is coming, but we know *who* is coming.'"[11]

Live today watching with hopeful anticipation for his return.

Reflections

- Remind yourself of some "It doesn't get any better than this" moments you have experienced, and give thanks.
- Whatever trials you may be facing, ask God to show you hidden treasures in your circumstances.
- Bring your hurts to Jesus, and receive his comfort and healing.
- Make sure your heart is prepared for his coming, for we know not the day or hour of his return!

Scripture

- Acts 17
- 1 Thessalonians 1-5

Memorize 1 Thessalonians 5:16-18

Always be joyful. Never stop praying. Be thankful in all circumstances, for this is God's will for you who belong to Christ Jesus.

Suggestion

Daily read aloud 1 Thessalonians 5:16-18. If you have recording equipment, record it, and listen to it as you travel to and from work or as you complete tasks around home.

Reflection Insights

_____

_____

_____

_____

_____

_____

_____

_____

_____

_____

_____

_____

_____

_____

_____

_____

_____

_____

_____

_____

_____

_____

II. RECONCILE WITH
YOUR REDEEMER

A testimony can result in life-transforming reconciliation.

*If anyone is in Christ, the new creation has come: The
old has gone, the new is here!* (2 Corinthians 5:17, NIV).

....

Paul preached the message of new life in Christ along the coast of the
Aegean Sea from Thessalonica to Berea, Athens, and all the way to
Corinth. When he wrote his first letter to the Corinthian believers a
few years after his letters to the Thessalonians, he appealed to his brothers and sisters in Christ regarding divisions in the church and warned
them about spiritual pride and sexual sin, among other issues. In his
second letter to them, he includes topics on forgiveness, generosity, and
reconciliation.

Paul emphasized that this transformed person we become, this new
creature, is from God, "who reconciled us to himself through Christ"
(2 Corinthians 5:18, NIV). Reconciliation is a powerful work of God in
his children, and he in turn gives us the ministry of reconciliation, the
task of reconciling people to him.

And all of this is a gift from God, who brought us back to himself through Christ. And God has given us this task of reconciling people to him. For God was in Christ, reconciling the world to himself, no longer counting people's sins against them. And he gave us this wonderful message of reconciliation. So we are Christ's ambassadors; God is making his appeal through us (2 Corinthians 5:18-20).

One of the best ambassadors of reconciliation that I know is my French friend Yori, whom I met at the first "Come to the Fire" conference. She arrived with my friend Rondy, and since one of Rondy's assignments was making announcements from the platform at each session, she and Yori sat on the front row. Yori reported,

Although I attended "Come to the Fire" to be with a friend and have a good time, God had an agenda! Never had I worshiped this way before. The presence of Jesus was powerfully felt in my soul; I was lifted heavenward! Every speaker was dynamic and anointed. God used the healing service to wrench my heart. As we were going through the motions of repentance and forgiveness, I heard a whisper:

"You have not forgiven your ex-husband."

I sobbed! "I sincerely believed that I had forgiven him, Lord! How can one know if he has truly forgiven someone?"

God taught me. You can forgive only when you are not expecting anything from the offender anymore. Searching my heart, it was clear that I was still expecting validation, amends, or recognition from my ex-husband. Since it was not happening, expectations were unfulfilled; anger was lingering underneath; and closure could not take place. In light of this, I had to reconsider all my past relationships. It was time to let go, renounce my expectations, and seek validation from my heavenly Father. Then, and only then, was I able to forgive. It was a place of freedom and rest.[1]

Two years later Yori was one of those dynamic speakers at "Come to the Fire" giving evidence of a "new creation" and details of her reconciliation-with-God journey. Yori says that although she had everything in life the world deems the most desirable to be happy, she was desperately searching for love and a sense of belonging. As she grew up, the basic needs of love, security, significance, and self-worth were unmet; therefore, she struggled with a poor self-image and the feeling that she was never good enough. She determined that if she could become successful with money and power, she would overcome her insecurities; and if she could find her Prince Charming, she would be loved and never feel lonely—so she thought. After she achieved her goals, she remained broken.

Yori followed her dream to be a professional ballerina; later she became an actress. Unfortunately, her early success had very little impact on her personal issues, and she realized a successful career was not the answer. She thought that Prince Charming would meet her needs, and the fairy tale began when she met an Italian prince but ended when he stepped out of her life because she was pregnant. Yori continues her story:

In show business circles, to expect a child without being married was not a big deal. So out of wedlock I gave birth to a daughter, found a nanny to care for her, and refocused on my career.

When I finally married, I was happy to commit to something that had meaning, especially since it appeared to be another fairy tale because my husband was an English lord. It was quite enchanting to become a part of the high society, a world of politeness and beauty where you met royalty. But as good as circumstances were, it was clear that I had fallen in love with the situation more than the man, and we divorced.

While acting in a play, I met my second husband, who was a famous French actor. We had a son. I was now the mother of two but more involved in the jet-set life than in the lives of my children. From the outside my life looked quite glamorous. From the inside, though, it was a different story. Once more my needs were unmet in a relationship, so I divorced again.

Husband number three was a billionaire. Now I was living the lifestyle of the rich and famous. We traveled in private jets. We had houses around the world. I could buy whatever I wanted—except satisfaction and rest for my soul.[2]

Yori turned to fortune-tellers, the occult, hypnosis, pills—and depression prevailed. After two failed suicide attempts, she decided to move to the United States. Read Yori's version of the story:

I wanted to flee far away from my problems to a place where nobody would know me, so I made the decision to move to the Unites States and leave my billionaire husband. I took my son, furs, jewelry, and pills and moved to America. My daughter remained in Paris. My third husband divorced me, and since I was at fault, I was left with nothing. Here I was in a new country and new culture with a new language, new people, no work permit, and no means to support myself. I had to start selling my furs and jewelry to survive. With no friends or plans and no way out, my fears worsened; so did my intake of pills. I began to have panic attacks and hallucinations. The pain was not only in my mind and soul now—it was in my body, and it was excruciating![3]

A neighbor extended friendship and eventually, through overtures of love, led Yori to faith in Jesus. Yori said,

One evening this lady shared with me how her life had been changed by Jesus. She told me things I had never heard before: I mattered to God but was separated from him by the things I had done; if I were to come to Jesus and tell him that I was not perfect, he would forgive me. I would be reconciled with him, and he would help me restart my life with a clean slate.

I wanted a clean slate, but I was raised in an environment where there is no such thing as "sin." It is in the dictionary but not in our vocabulary. Consequently, it took me a while to admit that I had messed up or to accept the idea that maybe there was a God. I finally asked this lady to explain to me how to reconcile with God. I am not going to pretend that I understood everything that she said. At this point, my mind was hardly functioning because of the pills, but I gathered one thing—God could do something for me right now, so I took the challenge and made a connection with God. I began reading the Bible, praying, and in time realized I was now completely transformed with different desires and priorities. Later I found a verse in the Bible that says, "Therefore, if anyone is in Christ, he is a new creation; the old has gone, the new has come!" (2 Corinthians 5:17, NIV). I was that new creation! God works in mysterious ways, and with him all things are possible. It was not enough for him to change who I was—he turned my life around, bringing about many other changes through reconciliation.

In reconciliation there is healing. I was at odds with myself, my family, men, people, the world, life. I could not imagine ever being reconciled with myself. I hated who I was and the way I lived my life. In the Bible I read a different story, one that says that I am wonderfully made by a God who loves me, a God who had a plan for my life, a plan to prosper me and not to harm me, to give me hope and a future (Jeremiah 29:11). When I saw myself so special in God's eyes, I was reconciled with myself.

I was reconciled with my daughter, my mother, and with men. You see, I was expecting a man to meet my needs. It is sad that I had to be at the end of my rope to find out that only God could meet all my needs. The good part is that it allowed me to finally meet the man of my life, a man who, like me, was reconciled with God late in life, and we have been married for twenty-three years.

Finally I was reconciled with life. The Bible became a love letter that helped me make better choices. Life is good now, not because I have a yacht, a Rolls-Royce, or my name in the paper—it is because my search for love, security, significance, and self-worth has ended because Jesus is enough.

Sometimes I wonder where I would be today if my neighbor had not loved me enough to tell me what I needed to hear. She was right; there is hope for the broken heart and the restless soul. I am a new creature today because of her testimony.[4]

Although Yori has the same body, her testimony reveals that she is a new person in Christ—dead to sin but alive unto God in Christ Jesus.[5] She's an Easter story on display for the resurrected Lord as she watches and waits for his return. She is strong and immovable, working enthusiastically for the Lord, for she knows that nothing she does for the Lord is ever in vain.[6]

Moments ago I had a message from Yori asking me to pray for her as she travels to Paris in a few days as Christ's ambassador. Where may God be leading you as his ambassador to tell the good news of reconciliation? Could it be to a hurting, broken, impossible neighbor, a family member, or someone you have yet to meet? Be alert—prayerful and watchful!

Reflections

- Allow God to search your heart; listen for his whispers. Is there anyone you have not forgiven?

- Ask God where he wants to take you as his ambassador. Perhaps it is next door or to a family member or coworker. Begin interceding in prayer for that person, and watch for opportunities to be Christ's agent of reconciliation.

Scripture

- Acts 18:1-17
- 1 Corinthians 15
- 2 Corinthians 3-6

Memorize 2 Corinthians 4:7, NIV

We have this treasure in jars of clay to show that this all-surpassing power is from God and not from us.

Suggestion

Locate a clay jar to place somewhere in your home or workplace to remind you of this scripture. Pause to look at it as you quote 2 Corinthians 4:7, and spend a few moments reflecting on what that verse means to you.

Reflection Insights

BEFRIEND AND
EXTEND HIS LOVE

I. WALK WITH ENLIGHTENED VISION

A prayer walk can change your heart and direction!

> *I keep asking that the God of our Lord Jesus Christ, the glorious Father, may give you the Spirit of wisdom and revelation, so that you may know him better. I pray also that the eyes of your heart may be enlightened in order that you may know the hope to which he has called you, the riches of his glorious inheritance in his holy people, and his incomparably great power for us who believe* (Ephesians 1:17-19, NIV).

I am a map reader and love to trace Paul's travels as I read the book of Acts. Paul concluded his second missionary journey in Corinth, then took a different route on his return to Antioch. He traveled to the Port of Ephesus and stayed briefly before sailing to Caesarea. From there he visited the church at Jerusalem and then went back to Antioch.[1] After spending some time in Antioch, Paul made his third missionary journey, strengthening believers along the way. Eventually he reached Ephesus, where he preached boldly in the synagogue for three months, then held daily discussions at the lecture hall of Tyrannus for two years.[2]

These hundreds of miles of travel and Paul's visits to many cities take only a few verses to tell, yet so much happened. Several years passed, and Paul was a prisoner in chains by the time he wrote a letter to the faithful followers of Christ in Ephesus. He told them of a God rich in mercy, reconciliation, peace, and forgiveness. He spoke of confident hope and prayed that the eyes of their hearts would be enlightened—flooded with light. I returned to Ephesians 1:18 today and asked myself some pointed questions.

What do you see, Patsy—a carpet that needs vacuuming, dust on the furniture, trash on the garage floor, weeds in the flower beds—or God's amazing world, hurting neighbors, confused children, a grieving community? All the above collided on what set out to be an ordinary day!

I'm one of those persons who flits from task to task. Just ask my husband, and he will tell you that I leave a trail behind everywhere I go. While vacuuming the bedroom carpet, I might notice that the furniture needs dusting. I will leave the vacuum cleaner in the middle of the floor and head to the laundry room for a dust cloth. En route back to the bedroom, I hear the mailman and decide to leave the dust cloth on the end table, while I scurry outdoors to check the mailbox. I discover a few weeds in the flower bed, and after opening the mail, leaving envelopes and catalogues on the kitchen counter, I take the junk mail to the recycle bin in the garage and notice the trash bags, reminding me of the weeds. Before pulling weeds, I see that the garage floor needs sweeping, so I open the garage door and begin sweeping away. With fresh air and sunshine flowing in and prediction of rain later in the day, I decide it's a great time to take a walk. Curtis comes home to find the garage door up, a few weeds in a bag on the driveway, trash swept into a heap beside a broom lying on the garage floor, mail strewn on the kitchen counter, a dust cloth draped over the living room end table, and the vacuum cleaner in the middle of the bedroom floor—but his wife is nowhere to be found. She's in the neighborhood, prayer-walking, beholding God's creation.

Even when I have every intention of prayer-walking my neighborhood, my thoughts can shift from one idea to another, or my mobile phone may ring, and I will talk nonstop, not noticing a thing along the way. Oh, yes—I see where I'm going. I have vision but little awareness of what's happening around me.

One morning I could have easily walked my neighborhood, unaware of a great tragedy that had happened a short time before. I noticed several cars parked down one street and made a decision to choose a quieter route rather than go that direction, thinking someone was having a brunch or social gathering with people coming and going. I observed a car slowly drive past me, then turn around. The driver stopped, rolled down her window, and asked if someone else in our neighborhood had experienced a robbery. She introduced herself as a new resident who lived on the other end of our subdivision and told me that they had already had a break-in. She was turning around because she saw a police car on the street that I had just passed.

We went back to the parked cars and saw a man standing on the street beside his truck preparing to make a phone call. She asked him if there had been a break-in. He gave us the heartbreaking news that his brother had committed suicide in his parents' home that morning. We gave him our condolences, and I quickly walked a few streets away to a neighbor who leads the hospitality and communication committee in our subdivision. She had already heard the news from a friend who lived across the street from the grieving family. Diana invited me in, and I asked her if we could pray together for our neighbors. I expected to stand by the front door to say a brief prayer; however, she headed to her living room sofa, knelt, and I dropped beside her, where we wept and poured out our anguish to God for this family and our neighborhood.

I then hurried home, drove to the market to purchase sandwich and fruit trays, and immediately delivered them with assurance that we were praying. I learned that the victim was a dearly loved, effective teacher at the nearest high school, and his wife was the principal of the middle school where our neighborhood children attended. This tragedy happened on a school day in the morning hours shortly before students made their way to a classroom devoid of their esteemed teacher who would never return. Our entire community was affected.

Since I am away from my neighborhood traveling many days each year and often don't read the newspaper or watch the news when I'm home, and because I was walking oblivious to what was happening around me, I could have missed learning of a mourning family just two streets from my home. My new neighbor's recent break-in had caused her to be alert. In God's timing, he broke into my oblivion and placed me right in the middle of where he wanted me to be. I knew he was calling me to pray for confused children, troubled teens, tormented families, and an entire grieving community. He put me on alert, causing me to pray more diligently and specifically for my neighbors and to watch with his eyes and greater focus as I prayer-walk the streets surrounding my home. Oh, I can't say there aren't days when my thoughts zigzag from thing to thing, and I return home to my vacuuming, dusting, weeding, and sweeping with vague remembrance of what I have seen along the way; however, one walk opened my eyes, putting a burden in my heart for my neighborhood, and I will never be the same. That walk changed my heart and direction.

Take note—I'm not recommending charging into a new task before completing the previous one. Recognizing my shortcoming has put me on guard. Not only am I working on a plan to help stay focused on each task before exploring another, but I'm also watching to see how this trait may be affecting my spiritual journey. While writing this, I'm reminded of Ephesians 4:14, which warns not to be blown to and fro by every wind of doctrine and new teaching. I love Ephesians, and today I decided to read the entire book in two versions. Although I determined to stay focused to see what God had to say to me from his Holy Word, within a few verses I burst into prayer and began to write my prayer from Scripture:

> Thank you, God, for enlightening the eyes of my heart and giving me a vision for my neighborhood. Continue imparting spiritual wisdom and insight so that I may grow in your knowledge. I pray that not only will my heart be flooded with light so that I can understand the confident hope you have given but also that I will be alert to others who are searching for living hope. I pray also that I will understand and proclaim the incredible greatness of your power for all who believe.[3] I thank you that in spite of my weaknesses I can come boldly into your presence because of Christ and my faith in him.[4] This gives me renewed hope for myself and my hurting friends and neighbors. I long for unity in the body of Christ, that we will walk worthy of your calling, be gentle and humble, and make allowances for each other's faults.[5]

This morning I continued to read and pray, moving from one translation to the other: *Precious Jesus, I pray that I will never bring sorrow to your Holy Spirit by the way I live. May my words bring encouragement and hope to those who hear them.*[6] It is my desire to stand firm, be alert, and make the most of every opportunity. In this respect I can see that my inclination to move quickly from one event to another may be a blessing! *Please, God—don't let me get so attached to completing my agenda that I miss yours! You have my permission to break into my oblivion at any time you desire. You made me and understand my weaknesses, but you do not intend to leave me there. Continue to show me where I need to make improvements, and give me the courage to tackle the breaking of entrenched habits. Thank you that you choose to use your followers in spite of shortcomings, and that includes me. Open my eyes to see my neighbors and the hurting world through your eyes. Give me your enlightened vision.*

Ephesians 6 reminds us that we are fighting not flesh and blood but evil powers in the unseen world. We are advised to put on the whole armor of God to resist the enemy in these evil days. We are also cautioned to be alert, stand firm, and keep praying. "Pray in the Spirit on all occasions with all kinds of prayers and requests. With this in mind, be alert and always keep on praying for all the Lord's people" (Ephesians 6:18, NIV).

Could this mean praying and staying alert during vacuuming, dusting, weeding, sweeping, as well as when reading God's Word and prayer-walking my neighborhood? If we heed this advice, no task or walk will be insignificant. Believe me—one routine walk changed my life forever! It gave me an enhanced awareness of the hopelessness that successful, respected individuals near me may be facing as they go about their professional assignments. It reminded me that streets of beautiful homes with lovely flower beds and manicured lawns do not guarantee protection from deep sadness and the pressures of life. I saw my neighborhood through new eyes. Yes, one sad morning walk changed my heart and direction, and my prayers for my neighbors intensified. The book of Ephesians has given me renewed hope as I pray for myself and others in the powerful name of Jesus!

"Now to him who is able to do immeasurably more than all we ask or imagine, according to his power that is at work within us, to him be glory in the church and in Christ Jesus throughout all generations, for ever and ever! Amen" (Ephesians 3:20-21, NIV).

Reflections

- Take a prayer walk daily the next two weeks.
- Ask God to point out specific ways for you to pray for your neighborhood.

Scripture

- Read Acts 18:18-20:38.
- Read the book of Ephesians through in one sitting; then read a chapter or portion of a chapter each day, praying as you read that "the eyes of your heart may be enlightened in order that you may know the hope to which he has called you" (Ephesians 1:18, NIV).

Memorize Ephesians 6:18 (NIV)

Pray in the Spirit on all occasions with all kinds of prayers and requests. With this in mind, be alert and always keep on praying for all the Lord's people.

Suggestion

Make a paper copy of Ephesians 6:18. Fold and carry it in your pocket. Frequently read it, and breathe a short prayer when waiting—

- for food at a restaurant or when riding the bus to work
- in the doctor's office or the checkout lane at the store.

Reflection Insights

II. EMBRACE THE WORLD
Epiphany encounters may open doors
to enlarge your borders.

"Everyone who calls on the name of the Lord will be saved." But how can they call on him to save them unless they believe in him? And how can they believe in him if they have never heard about him? And how can they hear about him unless someone tells them? And how will anyone go and tell them without being sent? That is why the Scriptures say, "How beautiful are the feet of messengers who bring good news!" (Romans 10:13-15).

The world is on God's heart, and he invites us to embrace his world one person at a time! We sometimes become aware of this through epiphany encounters.

Curtis and I along with our son, Kevin, wept in the sporting goods section while shopping for bicycles as he told us about an epiphany encounter he had experienced three days before. Kevin is the teacher of an adult Bible class that meets at his church every Sunday and had headed late Saturday evening to Kinko's to have copies of a handout made. Thirsty, he returned home by way of the neighborhood Kum & Go service stop to get a Pepsi.

As he parked near the entrance, he noticed a couple of vans outside and a crowd inside, which seemed unusual this late at night. They were gazing at his car. Kevin visits this convenience store often and could see the relaxed cashier through the window, which indicated this large group was not a problem. As he entered, one who appeared to be the leader of the group made a comment in jest about Kevin's car, which opened the way to an engaging conversation.

Kevin learned that Mike, a previous gang leader, had brought this group of former gang members from another state to sell cleaning supplies and interview people to find out what had made them successful. Mike shared fragments of his story; he had one time been in the drug culture, the leader of a gang, and had bullet holes in both arms to prove it. After becoming a Christian, he, like Saul of Tarsus, was radically changed. He began leading others to Christ and influenced many young adults to leave drugs, gangs, and destructive habits for a new way of life. Thus, this group was now spending a few minutes visiting with my son in Oklahoma as they drank coffee and soda pop preparing for their late-night drive back to their home state.

Kevin was disappointed that these new friends were unable to accept his invitation to come to church with him the next morning. He said it would have been a strange sight for anyone driving by to see a group of new acquaintances joining hands and praying together in the Kum & Go parking lot late on a Saturday night. After prayer, Kevin turned to Michelle, the female leader in the group, and gave her a hug, saying, "Since my wife's name is Michelle, I won't forget you."

Mike piped up: "Well, Kevin, have you ever been hugged by a black man?"

Kevin responded with a smile, "Not one with bullet holes in his arms!"

As he walked over to give Kevin a huge bear hug, Mike replied, "Then let's fix that right now!"

What happened next will forever be etched in Kevin's memory—and mine as I can envision it. One of the young men across the circle quietly said, "I've never been hugged by a white man," and another shyly added, "I haven't either." (I have a huge lump in my throat just writing about it.) Kevin jogged over to them and repeated Mike's words—"Then let's fix that right now!" After good-bye hugs and farewell blessings, Kevin slid into his car with visions of lives forever changed, including his.

I can only imagine his emotions as he waved and headed home to his sleeping family, remembering this epiphany encounter while looking forward to, in a few hours, worshiping the risen Savior who orchestrated it all. His Lord and Teacher clearly mandated that we love our neighbors, be witnesses to the ends of the earth, and go into all the world in his name, telling the good news and making disciples. His Spirit nudges us in creative ways to obey.

We had invited Kevin to go bicycle shopping with us because he had a vehicle large enough to transport a purchase. Curtis came home with a bicycle and set out for his first excursion around the neighborhood with an adventuresome smile, new helmet in place.

He wasn't gone five minutes before he returned, face and arms bleeding, still smiling. Hoping I wouldn't panic, he cheerfully said, "I crashed!" Loose gravel sent him back to the stationary bike for exercise. He never rode the bike again and three years later sold it in a garage sale for less than half of what he paid for it. Someone today is riding a bargain bicycle while Curtis pedals, going nowhere. God doesn't intend for us to remain stationary in our service to him—or even to reach out only to close neighbors. He often stretches us out of our comfort zone to carry his message.

I have had epiphany encounters that could have been arranged only by God, who invited me to move forward into uncomfortable territory. Even with the fear of a crash, I obeyed as I checked to make sure my spiritual armor and helmet of salvation were in place.

On a cold, blustery morning a few months after Kevin's divine appointment with Mike and friends, God opened an unexpected door as I walked laps in the mall. Since it was the Christmas season, the corridors were lined with temporary carts where attendants were preparing their stations for shoppers. I noticed a couple of girls busy at the sea salts counter arranging products, and I knew what would happen next—eager young salespersons would approach potential customers inviting them to try a sample of lotion. Shops were opening earlier than normal that day, and soon I would need to look straight ahead and put on my "I'm walking—don't bother me" attitude as I passed.

The next time I circled by the sea salt cart, I noticed a new attendant had arrived. She had short, blonde, very curly hair. As I went about my day later, visions of the sea-salt blonde remained, and in the middle of the night I sensed God whisper, *Next time you see her, allow her to give you a demonstration; then ask her how you can pray for her.* I didn't walk in the mall every day, but when I did, I watched for her. She was never there; then Christmas week I traveled.

A couple of days before New Year's Day I returned to walk in the mall, and my heart began to pound when I spotted her uncovering the cart. She was busy and didn't look my way, so I decided not to disturb her. I walked another lap as I prayed for courage and the right words, hoping she wouldn't be involved with another customer when I stopped with hands outstretched to invite her to give me a demonstration.

My prayers were answered. I began by saying that although I knew she approached strangers daily, it wasn't easy for me; however, I had noticed her one day before Christmas as I was walking. Her name was

Addy. I learned that she was from Israel and had come to America alone to study acting. She had traveled to Oklahoma from California to work during the holiday season and would be returning in a couple of days to resume her studies.

After asking how I could pray for her, I inquired if she would be working the next day. She didn't know, since each day she was given a different location and assignment. I left her with a hug, saying I hoped to see her again. The next day between my scheduled activities, I took my book *Simply Praying* with a note in a gift bag, praying that Addy would be at her cart. She was! A customer was walking away as I approached, and Addy moved toward me with a big smile. I gave her the book and a parting hug.

Strangely, it felt as if I were saying good-bye to a dear friend as I waved and walked away. Then I heard my name, turned around, and Addy was running toward me for another hug and more thank-yous. I tearfully left the mall, almost late for my next appointment. I still think of Addy often and pray for her and her family in Israel—and invite others to join me in prayer. I may never see this young lady again or meet her family, but I know God is answering prayer and orchestrating more divine encounters for this dear girl.

A few weeks later I almost missed walking through a God-ordained open door. I was in Ohio to speak at a retreat and accidentally dropped a bottle in my hotel room. It broke, and the contents splattered everywhere. I showed the housekeeper before going downstairs to breakfast. When I briefly returned to my room after the morning session, I saw that everything had been cleaned and put in order. As I scurried down the hall to lunch, the young housekeeper was cleaning another room, and I looked inside to give her a quick "Thank you." She stopped what she was doing and came out to ask in broken English what kind of conference this was. When I told her that it was a Christian ladies' retreat, she asked, "Catholic?" and looked puzzled when I replied, "No, Protestant." I asked her if she were Catholic, and she said she was Russian, raised an atheist.

She wanted to know more. In simple terms I explained to her that we believe we can confess our sins, ask Jesus to come into our heart and cleanse it, and that he will be with us and give us joy as we face each day's problems. I wasn't sure if she understood, but I asked if I could pray for her. We held hands as I prayed for Jesus to reveal himself to her; then I hugged her before heading for lunch.

As I headed to the dining room, a thought came to me that perhaps she could read English and that my book *Simply Praying* might guide her in what I believed was her heart search. I grabbed a copy from the book table, rushed back to the elevator, and found her still cleaning. She eagerly accepted the book, saying that she loved to read and could read English. When she saw my name on the cover, she excitedly pointed to it and then to me. This was another epiphany encounter! I wonder how many I have missed when I have been in my agenda mode, but I will be forever grateful that God opened the door for me to meet Julia, a Russian atheist.

I love hearing of current divine appointments and reading in the Bible about those of early Spirit-filled believers. Because of persecution, Christ-followers in Jerusalem were scattered throughout regions of Judea and Samaria telling the good news about Jesus everywhere they went.[1] Phillip explained Christ to the Ethiopian and baptized him—the first recorded African convert.[2] Peter, following his vision, went to the home of a Roman officer named Cornelius, preached Jesus to the Gentiles who had gathered, and witnessed the Holy Spirit working in all their hearts. Peter said, "I see very clearly that God shows no favoritism. In every nation he accepts those who fear him and do what is right" (Acts 10:34-35).

Following his conversion, Paul took the gospel to the Gentiles throughout Asia and into Europe. After Paul appeared before the high council in Acts 23, the Lord appeared to him in the night and said, "Be encouraged, Paul. Just as you have been a witness to me here in Jerusalem, you must preach the Good News in Rome as well" (Acts 23:11). Paul wrote of his intent to visit the Romans in his opening chapter to them and eagerly told them he wanted to work among them: "For I have a great sense of obligation to people in both the civilized world and the rest of the world, to the educated and uneducated alike" (Romans 1:14). The commission to take the message of Jesus to all remains today!

"Love one another."[3]

"Be my witnesses."[4]

"To the ends of the earth."[5]

How? By simply watching for divine encounters, walking through doors that God opens, and embracing his world one person at a time! The results: he will enlarge your borders, do his eternal work, and be glorified!

Reflections

- Conclude this month by watching for epiphany encounters.
- Enlarge your intercessory prayer list to include people from various cultures.

Scripture

- Acts 21-26
- Romans 1:1-17

Memorize Romans 10:9

If you confess with your mouth that Jesus is Lord and believe in your heart that God raised him from the dead, you will be saved.

Suggestion

Draw a picture to illustrate this verse. Add the words to the appropriate locations on your picture.

Reflection Insights

TRUST AND AWAIT THE SUPERNATURAL

1. PARTICIPATE IN WHAT SEEMS IMPOSSIBLE

A redeemed soul will increase your faith.

Since we have been made right in God's sight by faith, we have peace with God because of what Jesus Christ our Lord has done for us. Because of our faith, Christ has brought us into this place of undeserved privilege where we now stand, and we confidently and joyfully look forward to sharing God's glory (Romans 5:1-2).

Danny Velasco felt he had reached the pinnacle of his career as a make-up artist when his models appeared on the cover of *Vogue* magazine. Although he was living the life of the rich and famous, he was already deep into the drug culture. He first learned of Jesus from Wanda, a pleasant model with natural beauty who sang in the Brooklyn Tabernacle Choir.

One day she asked if she could pray with him before she left his salon. He scoffed and rolled his eyes as she prayed. She invited him to attend church and told him, "The day you call on the name of the Lord, he is going to set you free."[1] Danny had no intentions of attending her church or calling on her God because it was hard for him to believe that a man who lived two thousand years ago could have any effect on his life today. He rejected her words as some kind of fantasy and eventually lost his career, health, and identity and lived for years as a homeless heroin addict. His street life of drugs caused him to develop all kinds of apprehensions and left him malnourished with hepatitis A, B, and C.

Eventually voices began screaming in his head. One was accusing and condemning; another constantly spewed out filthy language; a third laughed uncontrollably. He started talking to those voices and admits, "I was a crazy man walking the streets of New York riddled with phobias, fears, and these voices screaming in my head."[2]

Danny was riding the subway one day when another drug addict said, "Man, you're going to die. There's a hospital at the next stop, and you better check yourself in." Since Danny didn't want to die on the streets, he went into the hospital and was admitted. They gave him medication to sedate him.

As he was regaining consciousness, Danny was confused, and the voices started shrieking again—all three at once. In the midst of the screeching sounds bombarding his mind, the sweetest voice whispered, "The day you call on the name of the Lord, He will set you free."[3] This is the way Danny tells his testimony at that point:

I screamed out, "Jesus, O Jesus, help me—you're my only hope!" At that moment the Spirit of the living God filled that room. He swept over me, was all around me. I knew he was touching me, healing me. Immediately all the voices stopped. I knew at that moment that God was real and that he had healed me and that he loved me. I knew I would never be the same again. Now years have passed, and God has brought me to Brooklyn Tabernacle, where I heard about the good news of Jesus Christ, and this is where I serve my Lord and my God and sing in the choir.[4]

In a video in which Danny gives his testimony, pictures of his past flash on the screen presenting the visual image of a hopeless man on the streets of New York City, face gaunt, skin clinging to bones, sunken eyes, a shell of a body. It's hard to believe that the man speaking his testimony on the DVD is the same person. He's a new creature indeed! Appearing healthy, smiling, hopeful, vibrant, he says, "All I wanted was to get out of a jam, but God had so much more in mind. . . . It's almost like a trophy, his trophy, saying, 'I can do this in a life.'"[5]

On the video Danny says, "The voices never came back, and that has been eleven years ago now."[6] Curtis and I visited Brooklyn Tabernacle Labor Day weekend 2010 and asked about Danny. Sadly, we learned that he had died—but his testimony lives, and he will be resurrected with a new body at the Lord's return.

Danny did not know that for months, maybe years, before he called out to Jesus, Wanda had the Prayer Band and thousands in their prayer meetings praying for him. Are you praying for someone who seems beyond change?

Curtis and I showed the video of Danny Velasco's testimony at a prayer gathering. Afterward a lady came to me crying. She pointed to the screen and said, "That was me—only worse." I had met this woman a few weeks before at a church dinner and at first encounter knew she loved Jesus and had a heart to share him with others. I would never have imagined her past if she and family members had not revealed how far into sin her rebellious path had taken her. Loved ones had prayed for her for years and probably doubted she would ever change—or even could if she tried.

Jenny, a classical musician, was headed toward Julliard School of Music, but her life choices led her down a totally different path, one of extreme destruction, and now she lives with great remorse over her years of sin and the scars that remain. This talented girl was raised in church, knew about Jesus all her life, and had praying parents and grandparents. She called on Jesus many times but left her place of prayer to make selfish, unwise decisions. Her sad story included unwanted pregnancies, abortions, drugs, theft, arrests, mental illness, eating disorders, multiple divorces, numerous suicide attempts, and, in her own words, "demons of evil within and without." Sadly, she was a slave to sin, a shell of a person, trying in her own power to keep the law, please her parents, be a good girl, break the bondage, but was living in a Romans 7 state—struggling with sin, defeated for years.

Today she is living in an Easter world, resurrected to new life in Christ—forgiven, obedient out of love, victorious, maturing in her Christian walk, and joyfully sharing her faith. Romans 8 is her testimony! Jenny is now living in freedom because not only has she confessed, repented, turned from sin, been forgiven, been cleansed, and been reconciled to God, but she is also being discipled through Christian counseling, accountability partners, group Bible studies, daily obedience, and her pastor's biblical teaching, replacing lies of the enemy with truth from God's Word, reading inspirational literature, sharing her story, calling on the name of the Lord in prayer, listening, and following his call. Jenny radiates Jesus even in the midst of today's trials.

Among other difficulties, Jenny is facing major cancer surgery. She is aware that God has spared her life many times and that she will have opportunities to share her joy and hope with people as she walks through these trials. Jenny's joy inspires me. She is a living example of one being dead to sin yet now very much alive by the power of the resurrected Jesus. "He personally carried our sins in his body on the cross so that we can be dead to sin and live for what is right. By his wounds you are healed" (1 Peter 2:24).

When faced with what seems to be an impossible situation, Jenny, Danny, and the apostle Paul's testimonies give me hope to keep praying, trusting, and believing for the supernatural.

In Acts 27 we read of the beginning of Paul's adventurous journey to Italy. Halfway through the chapter, the first-time reader must wonder if Paul will make it to Rome. In the midst of travel delays and violent storms, Paul encourages the crew and travelers with a message from the angel of God and in faith proclaims, "So take courage! For I believe God. It will be just as he said" (Acts 27:25). Before Paul traveled to Rome, he had already written in his letter to the Romans this assurance: "So now there is no condemnation for those who belong to Christ Jesus. And because you belong to him, the power of the life-giving Spirit has freed you from the power of sin that leads to death" (Romans 8:1-2).

Who are the impossible Dannys and Jennys in your life who need to hear that good news?

Reflections

- Spend this month focusing your prayers on one person who seems beyond hope. Envision him or her as healed, whole, a testimony of God's redeeming grace.
- Ask God to enlarge your faith, and pray with boldness.

Scripture

- Acts 27
- Romans 5-12

Memorize Romans 8:1

So now there is no condemnation for those who belong to Christ Jesus.

Suggestion

Find a way to celebrate this freedom each day this week as you say Romans 8:1.

- Sing a song of praise and rejoice in your salvation.
- Call a friend and share your testimony of joy.

Reflection Insights

_____

_____

_____

_____

_____

_____

_____

_____

_____

_____

_____

_____

_____

_____

_____

_____

_____

_____

_____

_____

_____

_____

II. SHARE YOUR FAITH
A transformed life will increase your faith.

Whoever has the Son has life; whoever does not have God's Son does not have life (1 John 5:12).

In Todd Phillips' book *Spiritual CPR*, he illustrates a point with a "what if" story. Suppose you are traveling alone late at night, come upon a tragic accident, and discover a mangled body on the ground with no sign of life. You nervously attempt to give CPR. Just before emergency help arrives, you sense a slight movement. Todd says the first thing you're going to do when you get home is call someone, and he claims that you would never get over such a significant event. He reminds us that although such emergency encounters may be rare, almost daily we encounter spiritual catastrophes—individuals who "possess no heavenly heartbeat, no eternal breath."[1]

We are the instruments God uses to get the message of Jesus' saving grace to the spiritually dead. We have the joy of telling others where to find eternal life and living hope. God wants us to make Christlike disciples in all nations. That's what Jesus told his disciples to do in Matthew 28:19-20; however, Todd says that we share our faith not only because Jesus told us to be his witnesses but also for the joy of it.

Jesus said to his disciples after talking to them about remaining in the vine and bearing fruit—

When you produce much fruit, you are my true disciples. This brings great glory to my Father. I have loved you even as the Father has loved me. Remain in my love. When you obey my commandments, you remain in my love, just as I obey my Father's commandments and remain in his love. I have told you these things so that you will be filled with my joy. Yes, your joy will overflow! (*John 15:8-11*).

Near the end of John's life, he said in his first letter,

We proclaim to you the one who existed from the beginning, whom we have heard and seen. . . . He is the Word of life. . . . We are writing these things so that you may fully share our joy (*1 John 1:1-4*).

When Todd asked a gentleman hunched over a mop at the church if his job had ever gotten boring or monotonous after thirty-five years, he wasn't prepared for the response. "My job isn't cleaning floors with this mop. My job all my life has been sharing Jesus with lost folks . . . This mop and bucket," he said, ". . . *that's my cover!*"[2] The janitor never got bored with his job, because he knew God had placed him there for a purpose, and that gave him joy. Todd reminds his readers,

Every time we pass up an opportunity to share our faith, we miss out on knowing the complete joy God desires for us. At the same time, those who need to know the truth remain in the darkness.[3]

I heard Todd tell his personal story in a message on sharing your faith. It wasn't his "It doesn't get any better than this" sermon, but it could have been! Before Christ, he was living out of wedlock, opening strip clubs, and dealing with grave emptiness. He was surprised one day to learn that a guy from his university drug days had become a Christian musician. Out of curiosity he called his college classmate at 2:00 A.M. one morning. He said that night after night he would call his friend collect, argue, hang up, call back, curse, call this new believer a liar, and scream that his Christianity was a joke.[4]

Todd reminds us not to give up on the person who seems the most disinterested because this friend had no idea he was getting through or that Todd was locating and reading every Scripture passage mentioned over the phone. The friend kept answering the phone, accepting the charges, listening—and Todd knew without question there had been a change—his college buddy was a new creature in Christ.

One passage in Scripture often used to present the gospel is "the Roman Road." The Roman Road has been used many years in various formats, but the core of the presentation consists of four scriptures in Romans:

- "Everyone has sinned; we all fall short of God's glorious standard" (Romans 3:23).
- "The wages of sin is death, but the free gift of God is eternal life through Christ Jesus our Lord" (Romans 6:23).
- "God showed his great love for us by sending Christ to die for us while we were still sinners" (Romans 5:8).
- "If you confess with your mouth that Jesus is Lord and believe in your heart that God raised him from the dead, you will be saved" (Romans 10:9).

If you feel you must have many scriptures memorized to lead someone to Christ, mark these four passages in your Bible, and share the joy. It is great news to know and to share with someone, "If we confess our sins, he is faithful and just and will forgive us our sins and purify us from all unrighteousness" (1 John 1:9, NIV).

We have a friend who is the successful pastor of a thriving church. His wife told me that if God could save her husband, he could save anybody—that her cowboy husband was the last one anyone thought would change. She described him as a bar brawler, a man who would start a fight without a moment's notice. He is another of God's "impossible" answers to prayer. And who would have ever thought that Saul, the persecutor of Christ-followers, would be converted? Do you suppose Peter or any of the apostles ever considered witnessing to him? In the final chapter of Acts after Paul finally arrived in Rome, he continued to boldly and joyfully proclaim the message of Jesus.

Is there someone you have given up hope of ever turning to Jesus, and even if he or she did, you seriously doubt Jesus could clean the person up and turn his or her life around? Saul, Danny, Jenny, Todd, Jim, Bud, Yori, and millions of others are proof that Danny Velasco's words are true: "Jesus saves us, cleans us up, turns our lives around, and he then adopts us into his family."[5] Share your faith and increase your joy as you extend hope to those who are broken and hopeless.

Reflections

- Record the Roman Road scriptures in your journal.
- Ask God to empower you to share your faith with someone.
- Invite an acquaintance to lunch, and be a silent witness for Jesus as you listen to his or her story.

Scripture

- Acts 28
- Romans 3:21-28
- 1 John

Memorize Romans 4:7-8

Oh, what joy for those whose disobedience is forgiven, whose sins are put out of sight. Yes, what joy for those whose record the LORD has cleared of sin.

Suggestion

Create your own memorization tool.

Reflection Insights

_____

_____

_____

_____

_____

_____

_____

_____

_____

_____

_____

_____

_____

_____

_____

_____

_____

_____

_____

_____

_____

_____

_____

SEEK AND RECLAIM RELATIONSHIPS

I. ASK FOR FORGIVENESS

A request may bring healing and restoration.

Since God chose you to be the holy people he loves, you must clothe yourselves with tenderhearted mercy, kindness, humility, gentleness, and patience. Make allowances for each other's faults, and forgive anyone who offends you. Remember, the Lord forgave you, so you must forgive others (Colossians 3:12-13).

In her book *I Love My Mother, But . . .* Linda Mintle, a marriage and family therapist, writes—

Every grown-up daughter must come to terms with the fact that she is still her mother's daughter. . . . But the relationship begins with a cry. In some cases, a wail. Excruciating pain and joy all mixed together. Birth is a metaphor depicting the bond between mother and daughter. It's a relationship that can be painful—and can also bring immense joy. And here's the really amazing thing: It affects every current and future relationship. That's why we have to pay attention to it and make it the best we can.[1]

When I recommend this book to others, I tell them it is a great resource for improving communication, handling conflict, setting boundaries, and bringing a healing balm to any relationship. One of the best examples I know of a dual mother-daughter, daughter-mother mending miracle is between Yori and both her daughter and her mother.

In August 2009 just before I was to fly home from a meeting in Tennessee, a group gathered for lunch with Yori and her daughter, Eve, who was visiting from France. I was sitting across the table from Eve and taking a bite of my sandwich when I heard her say, "The person who hurt me the most led me to Christ."

I looked up without responding; however, I wondered, *Is she speaking of her mother?* Eve then continued, "And she is sitting here beside me." I immediately glanced at Yori to see her reaction, but she did not seem disturbed by Eve's comment. They began to tell us their amazing story of reconciliation.

Eve, who was raised in Paris in a family of artists, tells her story:

My mother was an actress, but behind a very exciting life, she was paralyzed by fear and insecurity. When she was eighteen and pregnant with me, my biological father left her. I grew up with stepfathers who didn't give me attention or love, and I could see how much my mother had been destroyed by these disappointing marriages. She was hectic, depressed, and addicted to pills. Our relationship was poor, and I left home at seventeen.

At twenty I was feeling prematurely old and had already seen too much of life. I was a singer, had many "friends," was going out to clubs and drinking too much. People thought I was funny, but inside I had lost all hope. Eventually my mother left France with my half-brother, and once more I felt abandoned. Two years later my mother came to visit. I noticed how different she was and asked,

"Mom, what's happening in your life? You're not the same person. You seem happy for the first time!"

She began to talk about Jesus and what he had done for us. It was like an evidence for me; it was so real. I didn't know anything about Jesus. I just knew that what she had, I wanted. I was twenty-four and looked fine on the outside, but there wasn't one day I didn't think about killing myself. When she talked to me about Jesus, I felt like something was happening at the mention of his name and that this was the answer to my doubts and fears. I knew right away that he was the answer to the questions I had had for so long. I cried and cried, but for the first time my tears were tears of joy, not sorrow. That very night I gave my heart to Jesus and felt so much loved by him.

My mother asked my forgiveness for all that she had done or not done that had wounded me in the past. She wanted me to recall and name every hurtful thing so that she could specifically ask forgiveness for each one. I had always wanted her to acknowledge my suffering and pain. Each time a hurtful memory would come to mind, I would share with her, and she would ask my forgiveness. That cleansing process lasted two years. The wall that was between us crumbled. I felt loved by her and by my heavenly Father. I know this was tough on my mother but liberating for both of us. At last I had a mother who cared about me and became my best friend!

My perspective on life completely changed. I began to read a Bible, attend a church, and talk to Jesus. Seeing me so different, some of my friends gave their hearts to the Lord. I met the man who became my husband, and he also made a commitment to Christ. We now have two children who have been raised in the knowledge of our Lord Jesus Christ.

For eighteen years I have opened my home once a week to a group of people from all venues of life—seekers and believers from diverse denominations and backgrounds. Around a meal we discuss issues of life in light of the Scriptures. The evening always ends in prayer, and through it all we have seen many conversions. Jesus is my all—Friend, Counselor, Comforter, and Savior. I love him with all my heart and thank him for what he has done for our family.[2]

As the conversation continued at that luncheon, Yori told the story of her mother's visit to the United States after Yori became a Christ-follower. Yori tells the story:

My mother was a successful designer in France. I had the same conflicted relationship with her that my daughter had with me. When she came to visit, she saw that I was a different person, and she started asking questions. Every time I would pronounce the name of Jesus she would get up and leave. One evening she asked more questions. I started talking about Jesus, and she stayed. When I explained who Jesus is and what she needed to do to receive him, she didn't say anything. The next day I saw her coming down the stairs; she looked at me and started bawling. At the breakfast table she said, "Yori, I did what you told me to do last night, and I spent the night with God." She was close to seventy and thought her life was behind her; she is ninety-plus now and is not the same person. We have a loving relationship because of Jesus; she's the mother I always wanted.[3]

We finished the luncheon rejoicing at these stories of transformation in relationships. As Yori, Eve, and I parted, I told them, "I'm going to speak the same words to my daughter that you, Yori, said to Eve, telling her you wanted to hear everything you had done or not done that had hurt Eve so that you could ask specific forgiveness for each perceived offense." That opportunity came to me within a few days.

One week later I was having a Saturday brunch for my Lydia prayer group and had invited our ten daughters and daughters-in-law. When I had moved to Oklahoma City, I asked God to give me the names of five ladies to invite to join me for prayer. We started meeting at my home to pray together before I even had the boxes unpacked. For a year we had been praying for our families, churches, and the world. We had also been partnering with a Lydia prayer group in Vanuatu.

Of course, our children are always on our hearts, and we had been praying fervently for our children and those of our partner group in Vanuatu. My daughter made plans to come from Texas for this special event where we were meeting each other, many for the first time. This was a stretch for her with a four-month-old baby and two young sons. Her husband arranged his schedule to keep the boys, and she arrived on Friday with the baby. As we were standing at the kitchen sink that evening, I told her about seeing Yori and meeting Eve earlier that week. I relayed their story, and we talked, prayed, and cried together for hours.

Our deep conversations continued throughout the weekend and into the months that followed. She was able to attend "Come to the Fire" with me less than three months later, where she met and spent time with Yori and Eve. The friendship and prayer partnership of two mothers and two daughters who have been touched in eternal ways by each other continue with strong ties of love across the miles.

In the letter to the Colossians, Paul said he wanted believers to be knit together with strong ties of love. It is believed that Paul wrote the Colossian epistle during the two years he was under house arrest in Rome. He advises that God chose them to be holy people and to

- make allowance for others' faults; forgive offenses;
- live in love, peace, thankfulness;
- make the most of every opportunity;
- let all that is done and said be representative of the Lord Jesus.[4]

This is wise counsel for family relationships as well as between members of the family of God—the body of Christ.

Reflections

- Read Colossians 3. Allow God to examine your heart and motives. Ask his forgiveness for anything false or impure that he reveals. Then allow him to clothe you with tenderhearted mercy, kindness, humility, gentleness, and patience, giving you the willingness to make allowance for each other's faults and forgive anyone who has offended you.
- Next ask him to clothe you in love, which is what binds us together in perfect harmony, and allow the peace that comes from Christ to rule in your heart. Then give thanks!
- Leave your place of reflection and prayer quoting Colossians 3:16. Rejoice!

Scripture

Read Colossians.

Memorize Colossians 3:13

Make allowance for each other's faults, and forgive anyone who offends you. Remember, the Lord forgave you, so you must forgive others.

Suggestion

Meditate on a different phrase each day, and repeat it often throughout the day.

Reflection Insights

11. OVERFLOW WITH GRACE

A request may initiate renewed communication.

Above all, clothe yourself with love, which binds us all together in perfect harmony (Colossians 3:14).

At the "Come to the Fire" conference in 2011, Lanissa and I gave our unrehearsed testimony about the results of my asking her the question Yori had asked her daughter—"Will you tell me all the things I have done or not done that have wounded and hurt you through the years so that I can ask your forgiveness for each offense?" I was standing on the platform to lead a closing prayer session following the message by Aletha Hinthorn. Ladies were still standing under the crimson chiffon draped over two poles, representing that their sins had been covered by the blood of Jesus. I had just bowed under the covering myself with my dear Lanissa. I looked down at the front row; there sat Yori, and in an unplanned moment I began sharing the story about Yori's question to her daughter, Eve. When I glanced down the row and saw my daughter, all that God had been doing in our hearts flashed before me.

As I was speaking this unprepared testimony, I invited Lanissa to join me on the platform. I still don't remember what she said when she took the microphone to speak, nor do I recall all that I said during those vulnerable few minutes; however, scores of women approached us afterward, weeping and saying, "I know what I'm going to ask my daughter [son] when I return home."

Should you choose to make Yori's request your own to a son, daughter, spouse, family member, friend, or coworker, make sure you don't say, "*If* I've done anything to offend you . . ." The wording is important: "Please tell me all the ways I've hurt or offended you in the past, because I want to ask you to forgive me for each offense." As painful as the process may be, you must be prepared to listen without defending or interrupting. It's wise to prepare yourself in advance for such a confrontation. (See "Reflections.")

I must caution you that not every attempt at restoration results in mended relationships. Two brothers, both active leaders in the same church, had strained dealings with each other. One repeatedly made overtures at reconciliation, but his apologies were spurned. Both are now deceased, and I'm not sure they ever came to peace.

I had a similar situation in which a lady was offended by something that I said to her husband that was inaccurately relayed to her. Although the conversation had nothing to do with her, she began attacking me. I asked her several times, even pleaded with her, to forgive me, but she remained cold and continued to speak unkindly about me. After I moved, I frequently prayed that God would give her the grace to forgive and that she would have peace. She died of cancer without my knowing if I had been forgiven. Whether our overtures are received or rejected, we will know that we have sown seeds of peace and can experience peace in our own hearts because we have followed the counsel given in Romans 12:18: "If it is possible, as far as it depends on you, live at peace with everyone" (Romans 12:18, NIV).

Nancy Leigh DeMoss was devastated by some statements about her that from her perspective were unfounded and extremely damaging.

All she could think about was how wrong the other person had been and how deeply she had been wounded. This allowed resentful, vindictive thoughts to take root. She realized that she was beginning to believe lies of the enemy: "The damage cannot be undone. I can't let this go. I can't help the way I feel." The next morning she opened her Bible and began reading where she had left off the day before at Matthew 5 and 6. By the time she got to "But if you do not forgive men their sins, your Father will not forgive your sins" (Matthew 6:14-15, NIV), she realized she had to make a tough decision.

She said, "Now I had a choice. Would I continue to believe the lies, or would I embrace the truth? That's when the battle really started. My emotions wanted to hold onto the offense. I wanted to nurse the grudge; I wanted to stay angry; I wanted to somehow hurt the person who had hurt me. But in my heart I knew that choice would lead to bondage."[1]

Nancy knew that if she was going to walk in the truth, she had to relinquish the right to get even or to withhold love from that person. She knew she couldn't wait until she felt like forgiving, recognizing that if she obeyed, her emotions would eventually follow. Although emotional release did not come immediately after she willed to forgive, she continued walking in obedience and looking for ways to rebuild the relationship and invest in the life of the one who had hurt her. She confided,

> In the weeks that followed, my emotions gradually followed my will. The truth had countered the lies; my spirit was free. In time, God gave me further insight into the original situation; He shed light on why I had reacted the way I had and showed me some deeper heart issues that I had not realized needed to be addressed. I'm grateful that He loved me enough to orchestrate circumstances to bring those issues to the surface, and I thank Him for using that experience to make me more like Jesus.[2]

Amazingly, God never wastes an experience. He uses each one creatively to enrich our lives and make us useful in his kingdom.

No one seems to be sure who the chosen lady was to whom John was writing his second letter, but he had wise counsel for her and for us today:

> The elder. To the chosen lady and her children, whom I love in the truth—and not I only, but also all who know the truth—because of the truth, which lives in us and will be with us forever: Grace, mercy and peace from God the Father, and from Jesus Christ, the Father's Son, will be with us in truth and love. It has given me great joy to find some of your children walking in the truth, just as the Father commanded us. And now, dear lady, I am not writing you a new command but one we have had from the beginning. I ask that we love one another. And this is love: that we walk in obedience to his commands. As you have heard from the beginning, his command is that you walk in love (*2 John 1:1-6*, NIV).

Reflection

Has God placed someone on your heart to ask forgiveness? If so, first fortify yourself:

- Pray from Colossians 1 that—
  you will have the knowledge of God's will;
  you will go forward with his wisdom;
  you will respond with honor and please him;
  the results will produce every kind of good fruit;
  through it all you will grow and learn to know God better.[3]
- Also, pray that you will be strengthened with his glorious power so that you will have all the endurance and patience you need and that you will leave the place of communication filled with

joy and thanksgiving, knowing he has purchased your freedom, forgiven your sins, and enabled you to receive your inheritance and live in the light.[4]

- Read aloud Colossians 1:15-23. All this will prepare you to face words that may be painful to hear.
- After your conversation, find a place to be alone with God to process what you have heard.

Let the message about Christ, in all its richness, fill your lives. Teach and counsel each other with all the wisdom he gives. Sing psalms and hymns and spiritual songs to God with thankful hearts (Colossians 3:16).

Scripture

- Continue in Colossians
- 2 John

Scripture to Memorize: Colossians 3:17, NIV

Whatever you do or say, do it as a representative of the Lord Jesus, giving thanks through him to God the Father.

Suggestion

Say Colossians 3:17 each morning before getting out of bed, and make it your prayer. At bedtime quote it again as you reflect with thanksgiving on the day's events.

Reflection Insights

TOUCH AND ACCEPT THE BROKEN

I. INVITE OTHERS TO COME

A single invitation can reap eternal rewards.

Then he [Jesus] turned to the host, "The next time you put on a dinner, don't just invite your friends and family and rich neighbors, the kind of people who will return the favor. Invite some people who never get invited out, the misfits from the wrong side of the tracks. You'll be— and experience—a blessing" (Luke 14:12-14, TM).

Last night I attended a mission conference and heard the story of a Korean couple of Buddhist background who became Christians while living in New Zealand. They felt called to missions and were given a ministry opportunity in Singapore. The wife, whom I'll call Kim, was very shy and struggling with her insecurities and language barriers. As she was walking alone feeling insignificant and unworthy, she came to a lake and paused beside the water to pray. Kim conversed with God about her timidity and fear of speaking to strangers; she wondered how she could ever be effective for God in this new country. A big turtle splashed in the water, and she spontaneously said hello.

Kim jumped when a male voice behind her responded with a cheerful greeting. She had not heard the young man walking along the path. He thought she was talking to him instead of the turtle. Shy Kim walked toward him and asked his name. When he told her it was David, she replied, "That's a great name—it's in the Bible!"

Then she asked him if he was familiar with the Bible, and he said no—he was Buddhist.

Kim's ready response was "Oh, I was, too, until I became a Christian."

The conversation continued, and Kim asked for David's phone number so that he could be alerted to fellowship gatherings. She then gave this information to other missionaries who were planning social events. They in turn invited David to activities. He was a lonely student away from home and responded to the invitation.

For a year he continued to attend social gatherings and made friends. One day he told the group he was moving to Australia to enroll in another school. Fortunately, the missionaries had contacts there! After he had been in Australia for a while, he sent a text to the Singapore missionaries saying he would be on holiday the coming weekend and wondered if they had some interesting places to recommend that he visit. His Singapore friends connected him with missionaries in Perth, and he traveled to spend the weekend with them. He had a great time visiting in their home and seeing places of interest. On Sunday David attended church with them.

The seed that had been planted and germinating in Singapore for a year sprouted. David became a Christian that day. Two weeks ago, he sent a text to his missionary friends in Singapore reporting that his brother and mother had become Christians. He wanted the missionaries to know that he has friends who are moving to Singapore soon. They, too, will be invited to fellowship gatherings—and the story continues. A single invitation can reap eternal rewards!

In one of my small Lydia prayer groups, I became interested in how the other three ladies came to know Jesus. Each of their stories began with an invitation. The pastor's wife was an adult and successful businesswoman when she was invited to church by a friend. Although she had attended other churches before, it had been only a ritual. At the new church she heard the good news that she could have a personal relationship with Jesus. She fell in love with Jesus and totally committed her life to God. She is an effective Bible teacher and leader who boldly shares her faith.

The lady beside her became a Christian as a teenager. Her father was invited to church by a teen boy whose dad boarded his private plane at the hanger where Patty's father worked. Patty's father accepted the invitation, and the entire family went to church. The next Sunday, Patty's mother returned to church with the children and gave her heart to Jesus. Patty had never entertained the thought of going to college until the pastor planted that seed of hope. He would take the teens to a Christian college several hours away for special events and encourage them to continue their education there after high school. The vision flourished, and Patty graduated from that university and today holds a master's degree. She is a teacher in a large city public school and a faithful leader in her church. Her Christian husband is a gifted musician and plays in a praise band. Their daughter is a graduate of the same Christian university her mother attended and is a youth pastor. That teen boy's invitation to Patty's father continues to bear eternal fruit.

The third lady was a preschooler when she was invited to church for the first time. On the day that Sunday school workers stopped at their house to see if the children wanted to ride the bus to church, the parents, who were both alcoholics, were eager to grant permission. They were usually sleeping late with hangovers on Sunday mornings.

This friend shared that she could hardly wait to climb aboard the bus each Sunday to leave behind the chaos of home. The lady she sat beside during the worship service wore a fur coat and smelled wonderful. The four-year-old snuggled and felt loved under the dear lady's arm. Today, several decades later, this preschooler who was made to feel special at church is a public school administrator working on a doctorate and is the Christian education director of her church. Her son is a pastor, and her daughter is a leader in her church. I seriously doubt if the lady with the fur coat or those who drove the bus or the one who knocked on the door and extended an invitation to church has any idea of the outcome—and the story isn't over. It's true—we never know how far-reaching a single invitation will be.

Today I received a high school graduation invitation from Ariel, the granddaughter of a friend. I haven't seen her for a while, although I have prayed for her as she has courageously battled leukemia. I won't be able to attend this special event, but many family members will be there who have benefited from a neighbor girl's invitation years ago. Long before Ariel was born, her grandmother and grandfather, Wanda and Joe, moved to a new neighborhood. Wanda longed to find a church to attend but was too shy to go alone. One day a nine-year-old neighbor, Susie, came to her house and invited her to Sunday school. She said her church was having a contest and that she wanted to have the most visitors. Wanda said, "I wasn't too shy to go that Sunday because I had a reason to attend—I had been invited!"

Soon Wanda prayed at the altar of that church, and the following year her husband gave his heart to God. Wanda and Joe were the first in their family to become Christians. They began to pray for and witness to family members, and today, forty years later, four generations of believers are laboring for Jesus in many leadership capacities, including eight pastors and several in lay ministry positions. Today Wanda continues to pray for Susie and gives thanks for her special invitation.

I also had a life-changing invitation from a seven-year-old cousin, Daley, who was visiting our family the week our church was having revival services. One evening while we were waiting to leave for the service, she asked if I would like to go to the altar with her to be saved. I didn't know I needed to be "saved," but I thought if Daley needed it, I probably did too. Although she was only a couple of months older, she explained that she had watched people give testimonies after kneeling at the altar, and she had prepared hers. Then she offered to help me plan one. We memorized and practiced on each other. It took three nights before we got the courage to go.[1] Although I didn't understand it all at age seven, I realize today that was an awakening to my need of a Savior, and I'm grateful to my dear cousin for inviting me to join her at the altar.

The Scripture passages we have been reading throughout the previous chapters of *Simply Rejoicing* reveal invitations. When two disciples of John the Baptist asked Jesus where he was staying, he invited them to come and see.[2] Andrew invited his brother Peter to meet Jesus;[3] Phillip invited Nathanael to "come and see" Jesus of Nazareth;[4] and Jesus invited each of them to be among his chosen twelve. Even to Levi, the tax collector, Jesus said, "Follow me and be my disciple" (Luke 5:27). Jesus invited himself to be a guest at the home of Zacchaeus.[5] In a vision Ananias was invited to visit Saul on Straight Street: "The Lord said, 'Go, for Saul is my chosen instrument to take my message to the Gentiles and to kings, as well as to the people of Israel' . . . So Ananias went and found Saul. He laid his hands on him and said, 'Brother Saul, the Lord Jesus, who appeared to you on the road, has sent me so that you might regain your sight and be filled with the Holy Spirit.' Instantly something like scales fell from Saul's eyes, and he regained his sight. Then he got up and was baptized" (Acts 9:15, 17-18).

Any invitation God extends will be life-transforming and can precipitate a chain reaction.

Paul also extended invitations, and throughout his ministry to both Jews and Gentiles we see the results. Paul invited Timothy, Silas, and others to join him on his amazing missionary journeys. Lydia invited Paul and Silas to be guests in her home in Philippi, and a church was born.[6] The people on the Island of Malta and the chief official, Publius, welcomed Paul and those shipwrecked and invited them to stay on the island. The result of that invitation was that Publius's father and all the other sick people were healed.[7] In the final verses of Acts when Paul was in Rome under guard, he invited local Jewish leaders to come get acquainted,[8] and he welcomed all who visited him.[9] Some were persuaded by his message.[10] To the end, Paul was inviting people to come to Jesus. I am blessed and inspired when I read these biblical stories, because I know from experience that our invitations to others today can also have a powerful, far-reaching impact resulting in great joy.

Reflections

- Extend an invitation and rejoice as you watch God magnify the results beyond anything you could conceive.

Scripture

This would be a good month to catch up if you have gotten behind on the recommended Scripture reading.

Memorize Matthew 11:28-30

Jesus said, "Come to me, all of you who are weary and carry heavy burdens, and I will give you rest. Take my yoke upon you. Let me teach you because I am humble and gentle at heart, and you will find rest for your souls. For my yoke is easy to bear, and the burden I give you is light."

Suggestion

Find a pretty note card suitable for sending an invitation; write this verse inside. After you memorize the verse, put the card into an envelope with an invitation to a friend to spend some time together sharing stories from your spiritual journey. Enjoy rich fellowship as you tell each other about the best invitation you've ever received.

Reflection Insights

11. CULTIVATE LASTING FRIENDSHIPS

A caring friend will stretch you spiritually.

Rejoice with those who rejoice, weep with those who weep (Romans 12:15, ESV).

....

Whether we are receiving an invitation from the Lord or extending an invitation he has prompted, we will be astounded by what happens next. God still invites men and women to follow him, join him in his work, feast on his Word, and spend time with him.

A few days ago I was looking in past journals for something I knew I had recorded before Thanksgiving 2006. While leafing through the spiral notebook, I saw a long prayer I had written for a friend earlier in November that year. I was intrigued and began reading it, then praying with fresh fervor for my dear friend, whom I rarely see. I decided to call and leave the prayer on her voice mail. Since she is a busy executive, I didn't expect her to answer, but she did. I learned that when she awakened, she sensed God saying he wanted her to stay home and spend time with him that morning. She accepted his invitation, called her secretary, told her she would be coming in later, and thus answered my call. After I read the prayer to her, she requested a copy of it; then she shared an answer to prayer. Before we ended our phone visit, we prayed together for a major request that was on her heart.

Her heartache for a loved one prompted me to share with her another special prayer, an "A-Z prayer," written by one of my prayer partners in a time of emotional darkness, a prayer that lists alphabetically the ways God chose to reveal himself in the face of each heavy emotion. The story becomes complex at this point because of the way God took the threads of our spiritual journey and immediately began to weave them into the tapestry of many others. My friend read the A-Z prayer over the phone to the distraught loved one later that day.

The next day she spoke in a chapel service, presented the prayer, and made copies to distribute to many who requested it so they could in turn pray it for themselves or send it to someone else. The story will never end. Its multiple facets continue to unravel as they are woven into other hearts—hiding in places I will never witness. When God invites us to spend time with him or pray for another person, his purposes are beyond our comprehension.

Julie and Mike moved from Johannesburg, South Africa, to a horse farm in Tennessee near their children when Mike retired from the airline industry. At their new church Julie saw an announcement about a regional leadership conference and decided to go, hoping to meet people and become involved in local ministries. She came to one of my seminars, bought the book *Simply Praying*, and invited a group of ladies to pray and study the book with her.

When Mike decided the horse farm was too much work, they sold it and moved to a golf community in another town. Julie began inviting ladies to prayer teas at her new home, using *Simply Praying* as a resource. When she learned that I would be speaking at a ladies' retreat nearby, she placed an empty chair at the table to represent me, and they prayed for the retreat. The women's ministries director at her church welcomed the idea and once a month planned a prayer event to pray for me and the director of the retreat, who had recently joined their church staff.

I was intrigued when I learned they were planning a prayer picnic a couple of months before the scheduled retreat, reminding me that God is not out of creative ways to unite his followers in prayer. When I arrived at the conference center, Julie at once enthusiastically introduced me to her new friends, who already felt as if they knew me—and they did. Prayer does that!

A few weeks ago I was invited to speak at Mike and Julie's church, and they opened their lovely home for me to stay with them. As we drove along the streets of their community, Julie would point and say, "That's my dentist's office; I invited his wife to my last prayer tea, and she came!" Then Julie would motion toward a house in her neighborhood and remark, "She comes to my prayer gatherings," or "I met the lady down that street and invited her to my next prayer tea."

Through the years, Mike and Julie have led Bible studies together in their home. I was spellbound at dinnertime when they shared God stories from adventures in Africa and various states of America resulting from these meetings. At one of their Bible studies several years ago, an airline pilot, Tom, started coming with his wife. Tom and Lil had witnessed a car accident ahead of them involving their two daughters; one daughter was killed, and they were dealing with great pain. Tom was unfamiliar with the Bible; another pilot in the Bible study encouraged him to look in the bedside table of his hotel room when he traveled, and he would find a Gideon-placed Bible to read. On his next flight Tom was telling his copilot about the new Bible study he was attending. His Christian copilot sensed that Tom's heart was ready and asked him if he would like to pray to receive Jesus into his life.

Before the copilot began leading Tom in the sinner's prayer, he grabbed Tom's hand. Everyone in the Bible study group was elated when Tom told them of his newfound faith and chuckled when he added, "I was hoping the flight attendant wouldn't open the door to the cockpit and catch us holding hands!" Tom and Lil continue to serve God victoriously, inviting others to the Savior. Whether at the church altar or in mid-air, at a kitchen table or kneeling beside your bed, sitting at a well or on the road to persecute Christians, at a tax collector's booth or in a fishing boat, the invitation from the Master is "Come, follow me."[1]

A single invitation can bear an eternal harvest! Accept divine invitations. Extend divinely inspired invitations, and receive infinite blessings—both seen and unseen.

In Luke 14 Jesus uses some form of the word "invite" a half-dozen times in the first fourteen verses. Jesus was eating dinner on the Sabbath day in the home of a leader of the Pharisees. Everyone was watching him closely. He healed a man whose arms and legs were swollen. He taught about humility. Then he boldly said to the host, "When you put on a luncheon, or a banquet . . . invite the poor, the crippled, the lame, and the blind. Then at the resurrection of the righteous, God will reward you for inviting those who could not repay you" (Luke 14:12-14).

Reflections

Invite others, one and all, rich and poor, old and young, the needy and lost, to come—

- to your Bible study or prayer group
- to attend church or a Christian concert with you
- to an evangelism tea or social gathering with purpose
- to _____ [You fill in the blank.]

Invite others to come to Jesus, the poor in spirit, those blind and crippled by sin, the weary and heavy-laden—expecting nothing in return—and be blessed by eternal, heavenly rewards.

Scripture

All passages are repeated from previously recommended reading.

- John 1
- Luke 5, 6, 14, and 19
- Acts 9, 26, and 28
- Romans 12

Memorize

Review previously memorized scripture.

Reflection Insights

_____

_____

_____

_____

_____

_____

_____

_____

_____

_____

_____

_____

_____

_____

_____

_____

_____

_____

_____

_____

_____

_____

_____

TREASURE AND DELIGHT IN THE TRUTH

I. SURRENDER TO THE LIVING WORD

A scripture has the power to penetrate and reveal truth.

> *The word of God is alive and powerful. It is sharper than the sharpest two-edged sword, cutting between soul and spirit, between joint and marrow. It exposes our innermost thoughts and desires. Nothing in all creation is hidden from God. Everything is naked and exposed before his eyes, and he is the one to whom we are accountable* (Hebrews 4:12-13).

God's words are powerful! Marilyn Feinberg correctly proclaims that his words contain unfathomable power: "In less than 250 words, God spoke the stars, planets, solar systems, galaxies, heavens, earth, clouds, seas, lakes, puddles, cliffs, dunes, caverns, twigs, petals, giraffes, zebras, polar bears, flamingos, puppies, the human race into existence. If God can do so much with so few words, then I can't afford to miss a single one."[1] She poignantly adds, "As demonstrated in creation and throughout the Bible, the words of God are life, they bring life, they instill life, they bring back to life. His words come alive not just in our minds but in our hearts as a holy reverberation of transforming power."[2]

When reading the Bible, watch carefully for words spoken by God, whether they come through visions, angels, a burning bush, fire on the mountain, a voice from heaven, or Old Testament prophets. "Long ago God spoke many times and in many ways to our ancestors through the prophets" (Hebrews 1:1).

The prophet Jeremiah recorded God's powerful proclamation: *"Does not my word burn like fire?"' says the* LORD. *'Is it not like a mighty hammer that smashes a rock to pieces?"'* (Jeremiah 23:29).

God's mighty Word is proclaimed through the teachings of his Son, Jesus Christ, in the New Testament Gospels, and when we pay close attention to his words, they will burn within us. After Jesus joined two of his followers on the road to Emmaus, walked along with them, explained from the Scripture writings of Moses and the prophets the things concerning the Messiah,[3] broke bread with them, then left, their eyes were opened, and they said to each other, "Didn't our hearts burn within us as he talked with us on the road and explained the Scriptures to us?" (Luke 24:32).

Near the conclusion of the Sermon on the Mount in Matthew's Gospel, Jesus compared a person who hears his words and puts them into practice to a wise man who built his house on a rock. The house built on a rock was able to weather the stormy wind and rising flood because it was built on a firm foundation. We can endure the storms of life if we wisely heed the words of Jesus and build our life upon the foundation of his teachings and the truths revealed through the Holy Spirit.

In the upper room on Jesus' last night with the disciples before his crucifixion, he spoke to them about the work of the promised Holy Spirit, whom he called "the Spirit of truth."

I will send you the Advocate—the Spirit of truth. He will come to you from the Father and will testify all about me (John 15:26). *When the Spirit of truth comes, he will guide you into all truth. He will not speak on his own, but will tell you what he has heard. . . . He will bring me glory by telling you whatever he receives from me. All that belongs to the Father is mine; this is why I said, "The Spirit will tell you whatever he receives from me"* (John 16:13-15).

We dare not miss a word of truth from God the Father, Son, and Holy Spirit recorded in the Bible. All of holy Scripture is divinely inspired; it should be read reverently and prayerfully with a heart open to receive its correction, instruction, and promises.

All Scripture is inspired by God and is useful to teach us what is true and to make us realize what is wrong in our lives. It corrects us when we are wrong and teaches us to do what is right. God uses it to prepare and equip his people to do every good work (2 Timothy 3:16-17).

The Word of God is alive, powerful, and revealing. Unless we allow God's Word to expose our true nature, we may live in blindness to our selfish motives, unhealthful desires, uncontrolled emotions, unwholesome relationships, unholy ambitions, and deceitful thoughts. Mark Batterson in his book *Soul Print* says, "Most of us live our entire lives as strangers to ourselves. . . . Our true identities get buried beneath the mistakes we've made, the insecurities we've acquired, and the lies we've believed."[4] Thus, he says we spend emotional, relational, and spiritual energy trying to be who we are not, which amounts to "forfeiting our spiritual birthrights."[5] Batterson concludes that if you want to know yourself, you have to look to God for your true identity, "which is made up of the things that are invisible to everyone except the All-Seeing Eye. And this is where the Holy Spirit plays such a vital role in your life. Until you see yourself through his eyes, you'll never get a vision of who you can become. The key to self-discovery is allowing the one who knit you together in your mother's womb to reveal things you do not and cannot know about yourself without his revelation. God knows you better than you know yourself, because he designed you, so if you want to get to know yourself, you've got to get to know God."[6]

God knows things about us that we could never figure out on our own. He reveals truth to us through his Holy Word and through his Son, Jesus, the Word who became flesh,[7] the One and Only who is the way, the truth, and the life.[8] Jesus proclaimed: "No one can come to the Father except through me" (John 14:6). He said to the people who believed in him, "You are truly my disciples if you remain faithful to my teachings. And you will know the truth, and the truth will set you free" (John 8:31-32). In Jesus we can know truth, be set free, have the assurance of eternal life, and receive the power to live a holy life—victoriously.

I have found this to be true, and I long for my offspring to know truth, freedom, and victory in Christ. I often pray for my family from Stormie Omartian's books on the power of praying using Scripture as a foundation.

I was caring for my son and daughter-in-law's three girls while they were traveling and asked God to give me a creative way to have bedtime prayers with them. I wanted the time to be special, and he gave me an idea. I spent time with each one, privately sitting on her bed with Stormie Omartian's book *The Power of the Praying Parent* in my lap.

Kiersten was the first child ready to be tucked under the covers. I told her that I often pray prayers for her from that book, changing the wording to fit a grandmother's prayer. I asked her to pick a chapter title from the table of contents, and I would pray the prayer at the end of that chapter for her. She carefully scanned all the way to chapter 17 and with conviction said that this was the one she needed.[9]

Then she began to explain that she hears lots of bad language at school that gets into her mind, and she doesn't want to say those words. She confessed that even when she doesn't speak them aloud, she sometimes thinks them, and that troubles her. Next she poured out her heart about another issue. She said she was trying always to be truthful without hurting someone's feelings, and she gave an example of something that had happened at school that week. A friend with new colorful socks cheerfully asked Kiersten if she liked them. Kiersten said, "I knew she wanted me to be excited and say yes, so I did." I could sense Kiersten's struggle because she added, "Although I didn't like them for myself, I really didn't lie, because if she liked them, I liked them for her." Kiersten was wrestling with what it means to speak truth and expressed a desire that her words be pure. (I can relate to this dilemma of how to be both tactful and truthful.) I added Kiersten's name to Stormie's printed prayer, which targeted Kiersten's need, and she heard me pray a prayer that included these words:

> I pray that Kiersten will hide your Word in her heart so that there is no attraction to sin—that she will run from evil, from impurity, from unholy thoughts, words, and deeds, and that she will be drawn toward whatever is pure and holy. Let Christ be formed in her, and cause her to seek the power of your Holy Spirit to enable her to do what is right.[10]

Before I left her room, Kiersten showed me a special notebook of prayers she had written, honest words from the heart of a sixth grader. My heart was singing as I said good night and turned off the light.

Eight-year-old Makaila was awaiting me in her bed, and she chose the chapter "Identifying God-Given Gifts and Talents."[11] Scripture was scattered throughout, and other verses were quoted at the end of the prayer. Today I have prayed again one paragraph from that beautiful prayer:

> Your Word says, "Having then gifts differing according to the grace that is given to us, let us use them" (Romans 12:6). As she recognizes the talents and abilities you've given her, I pray that no feelings of inadequacy, fear, or uncertainty will keep her from using them according to your will. May she hear the call you have on her life so that

she doesn't spend a lifetime trying to figure out what it is or miss it altogether. Let her talent never be wasted, watered down by mediocrity, or used to glorify anything or anyone other than you, Lord.[12]

Following the prayer, "Weapons of Warfare" were listed: Romans 11:20; Ephesians 4:7; 1 Peter 4:10; James 1:17; and 1 Corinthians 1:4-7. Praying from God's Holy Word is an effective way to lift our petitions to him.

After a precious time of prayer with both Kiersten and Makaila, I headed across the hall to Marissa's bedside. She quickly chose a prayer from the beginning of the table of contents, thrust the book back into my hands, and said honestly, "I need this one!" It was a bold prayer and one I probably wouldn't have prayed aloud in her presence had she not chosen it. That prayer also contained scripture throughout and following. This private moment alone with Marissa and God gave us an opportunity for transparent conversation, and I got a glimpse into her tender heart with insight for future prayers.

I have chosen special passages of Scripture to pray for each family member and claim promises for them. Mark Batterson says, "By the most conservative estimates, there are more than three thousand promises in Scripture. By virtue of what Jesus Christ accomplished on the cross, every one of them belongs to you. Every one of them has your name on it."[13] Meditate on God's promises, and circle them in prayer. Surrender to the living Word, and allow him to permeate your heart, reveal truth, and infuse hope. Look into the pages of the sacred book for words of life, and share them with others.

Reflections

- As you read the Bible this month, do it with intensity, listening carefully for truth God wants to reveal to you.
- Wait in his presence until you have the assurance of eternal life.

- Tell him of your bondage; then ask him to reveal ways he wants to set you free.
- All this will prepare you for Part II of this month's reading.

Scripture

Begin reading the book of Hebrews contemplatively.

Memorize Psalm 119:103-105

How sweet your words taste to me; they are sweeter than honey. Your commandments give me understanding; no wonder I hate every false way of life. Your word is a lamp to guide my feet and a light for my path.

Suggestion

Put a jar of honey, a Bible, and a flashlight in a small basket and place it on your kitchen counter along with three cards, one for each of the verses. Write a different verse on each card, and memorize the verses in any order you choose.

Reflection Insights

_____

_____

_____

_____

_____

_____

_____

_____

_____

_____

_____

_____

_____

_____

_____

_____

_____

_____

_____

_____

_____

11. DESIRE A HOLY HEART
The truth will cleanse, free, and heal.

Sanctify them by the truth; your word is truth. . . .
For them I sanctify myself, that they too may be truly
sanctified. My prayer is not for them alone. I pray also
for those who will believe in me through their message
(John 17:17-20, NIV).

The words of John 17:17-20 were spoken by Jesus at the conclusion of his high priestly prayer to the Father. The *New Living Translation* of verse 17 says, "Make them holy by your truth." Peter, who would have heard Jesus' prayer, gave this call to holy living: "You must be holy in everything you do, just as God who chose you is holy. For the Scriptures say, 'You must be holy because I am holy'" (1 Peter 1:15-16). These are strong words! How can it be?

A. Paget Wilkes lists what he calls the sevenfold work of sanctification[1] after quoting Hebrews 12:14: "Follow peace with all men, and holiness, without which no man shall see the Lord" (KJV).

I suggest you pause following each of these teachings and spend a day praying, probing the Scriptures, and allowing the Holy Spirit to do a deep, refining work.

1. Through Christ Jesus our conscience can be purged of dead works and evil deeds—purified and renewed:

The blood of Christ will purify our consciences from sinful deeds so that we can worship the living God. For by the power of the eternal Spirit, Christ offered himself to God as a perfect sacrifice for our sins (Hebrews 9:14).

2. Our will can be surrendered and crucified with Christ—transfigured:

I have been crucified with Christ and I no longer live, but Christ lives in me. The life I now live in the body, I live by faith in the Son of God, who loved me and gave himself for me (Galatians 2:20, NIV).

3. Even the passions and desires of our heart can be nailed to the cross:

Those who belong to Christ Jesus have nailed the passions and desires of their sinful nature to his cross and crucified them there. Since we are living by the Spirit, let us follow the Spirit's leading in every part of our lives (Galatians 5:24-25).

4. Our affections can be circumcised and those things taken from our hearts that deflect our love and mar our wholehearted devotion to the Lord.[2]

The LORD your God will circumcise your hearts . . . so that you may love him with all your heart and with all your soul, and live (Deuteronomy 30:6, NIV).

When you came to Christ, you were "circumcised," but not by a physical procedure. Christ performed a spiritual circumcision—the cutting away of your sinful nature (Colossians 2:11).

Consecration and devotion to God are not difficult if we are in love with him as he is with us.

5. Our imaginations can be steadfastly established and fixed upon God.

Wilkes says that "imagination, the faculty that is always forming and giving shape to things that do not exist, is the stronghold of unbelief."[3] He explains that we imagine God's way is difficult and his will unbearable; we imagine trouble that never comes; unbelief whispers that sin is too strong and the price too costly.[4] Wilkes quoted the prophet Isaiah: "Thou wilt keep him in perfect peace, whose mind is stayed upon thee" (Isaiah 26:3, KJV). He says the word "mind" in that verse means imagination in the original[5] and affirms, "Yes, God can sanctify even our imaginations and cast out all unbelief, so that we shall walk not according to the imagination of our own evil hearts but according to his 'law,' his 'voice,' and his 'word.'"[6]

6. The thoughts of our mind and our attitudes can be renewed when we seek the mind of Christ:

Let this mind be in you, which was also in Christ Jesus (Philippians 2:5, KJV).

Since you have heard about Jesus and have learned the truth that comes from him, throw off your old sinful nature and your former way of life, which is corrupted by lust and deception. Instead, let the Spirit renew your thoughts and attitudes. Put on your new nature, created to be like God—truly righteous and holy (Ephesians 4:21-24).

7. Our memory can be healed.[7]

Wilkes names three things that can change, heal, and keep it fresh:

1. The Word of God. "These things have I told you that . . . ye may remember" (John 16:4, KJV).

2. The Spirit. "The Holy Ghost . . . shall . . . bring all things to your remembrance" (John 14:26, KJV).

3. The blood of Jesus. "This do in remembrance of me" (Luke 22:19, KJV).[8]

Wilkes adds:

How can we remember unless we read and meditate on His Word? How can we remember unless His blessed Spirit be the "Divine Remembrancer"? . . . How shall He keep us in remembrance unless the blood has first been applied to cleanse and heal?[9]

Do you hunger and thirst for a holy heart? Do you desire it with a passionate longing? The living Word has the power to do a redemptive, cleansing work in every yielded heart. Dennis Kinlaw tells of a colleague of his who found Christ as a young person, was called to preach as a teen, and became a successful pastor. The man said that as he preached and worked in the church, he began to have an emptiness in his heart. One day he went to his study, locked the door, and fell with face to the floor, praying, "Lord, if this is all there is, I don't know if it's worth it or not. Isn't there something you can do for me, so that I can have the power to live the Christian life with some kind of effectiveness, joy, and meaning?"[10]

At that point, he said, "It's as if I were a briefcase. God picked me up and turned me upside down, then he began to shake me. And as he shook, I was appalled at what began falling out of my life. Impurity, pride, arrogance, unbelief, all of the evidences of carnality began to fall out there. He shook me until I wondered if there would be anything left. Then it was as if he stopped shaking and turned me right side up. He poured himself in and filled me completely. That fiery, holy Presence just permeated every corner of my being."[11] Not only was this pastor's heart turned upside down and the discord gone, but people began to notice the change and ask him what had happened.

Dr. Kinlaw says, "I've observed that the divided heart is a common experience among Christians. However, it is not the way that the New Testament calls us to live."[12] He states that all great revivals have started "when God's people began to seek 'the mind of Christ.' When they set aside the normal human way of thinking about the world and allowed Christ to direct their lives, the world has been turned upside down" (Acts 17:6).[13]

As a result of a cleansed holy heart, truth, blessing, goodness, and light can flow from us, penetrating a world of shadows, turning the world upside down as those early Christ-followers did after experiencing Pentecost!

Reflections

- Return to Paget Wilkes' sevenfold steps to sanctification.
- Meditate on each one, praying those Scriptures into your own heart.

Scripture

- Continue reading the book of Hebrews.
- Prayerfully reread all the Scripture verses quoted in this chapter.

Memorize Hebrews 4:16

So let us come boldly to the throne of our gracious God. There we will receive his mercy, and we will find grace to help us when we need it most.

Suggestion

Repeat this verse on your knees, bowing before God in prayer, sitting reverently with face upward, standing with arms outstretched in praise, while walking and rejoicing with a holy heart.

Reflection Insights

_____

_____

_____

_____

_____

_____

_____

_____

_____

_____

_____

_____

_____

_____

_____

_____

_____

_____

_____

_____

_____

SHINE AND BRIGHTEN A DARK WORLD

1. RESPOND TO THE QUESTION

A question may evoke a soul-searching response.

After breakfast Jesus asked Simon Peter, "Simon son of John, do you love me more than these?" "Yes, Lord," Peter replied, "you know I love you." "Then feed my lambs," Jesus told him (John 21:15).

....

I sometimes answer God's question with a question, although I'm convinced he wants a definitive response. I stall, ponder, analyze, soul-search, hedge, and ask for an explanation, although he knows, and I do, too, that deep down inside I'm trying to divert the dialogue to some topic less probing. God's questions penetrate and won't go away unanswered. Oh, we may remain silent; however, he knows our answer whether or not we speak it. No response becomes an answer.

He also knows if we're responding with shallow words. It is for our own benefit that God petitions us to answer his questions, and words alone are not enough. He searches and knows our hearts and motives better than we do. He continued to ask Simon Peter the same question three times. Simon's first two answers were the same: "Yes, Lord, you know I love you."[1] The third time Peter said, "Lord, you know everything. You know that I love you" (John 21:17). With these pointed questions, Jesus was commissioning and preparing Simon to become Peter, the rock, a spokesman for the gospel message to extend his kingdom. When God asks a question, he is getting ready to reveal something important to us that may include truth about ourselves or insight into a future assignment.

In the wee hours this morning when I was wide awake from 1:30 A.M. until 6:00 A.M., God surprised me with a question. Well, maybe it wasn't a total surprise, because in retrospect I can see that he has been leading me there for a couple of weeks. It started with a sermon I heard on suffering believers in areas hostile to Christians. The topic of suffering for Christ has been reinforced through Scripture, books I've been reading, and my quiet time with him. Twelve hours later, I'm still struggling with his question: "Are you willing to suffer?"

Everywhere I went today the question was front and center. The Bible study at church pointed to it; the sermon addressed it; even the worship music and prayer time called attention to this ever-present inquiry from my Lord. When I read his garden of Gethsemane prayer, I truly believe Jesus understands my human struggle with this question.

On Palm Sunday I visited my son's church and heard him teach his young adult Bible class. He was concluding a series on the prayers of Jesus and presented a dynamic lesson on Christ's Gethsemane prayer. I have returned to that agonizing prayer of my Savior to Abba Father;[2] it's helping me find words to pray as I sincerely probe my own heart for a truthful answer.

This is not the first question God has asked me, nor do I expect it to be the last. Tuesday, March 22, 2011, I was flying from Oklahoma City to Nashville for several events. That night I was scheduled to speak at a prayer gathering, and throughout the flight my mind had been focused on that meeting. As the plane approached the landing runway, my thoughts turned toward renting a car and going to visit my mother at the assisted living facility where she lives near Nashville before heading to my speaking engagement.

God interrupted my deliberations with an abrupt question: *What are you expecting to happen tonight?* Although I knew he was probing for a definite transparent answer, my response was "Well, I expect you to be there."

I was caught off guard with his next question: *Are you expecting a miracle?*

Stalling, I inquired, "What do you mean by a miracle? I see miracles every day; I'm looking for them. Do you mean a marvel that everyone, even doubters, will witness and declare miraculous?"

He knew I was playing word games. I wanted to exclaim, "Yes, I *am* expecting a miracle to happen at the prayer meeting tonight even though I have never been to this historical church, am meeting most of these people for the first time, have no idea how many will be there or what their usual format is—but I know you, the miracle-working God! Yes! Yes! Yes! I am expecting a miracle—many miracles—this very night!"

I indeed did see miracles that night, the next day at a radio interview, the following three days at a songwriters' retreat, and in the two teen Lydia prayer groups where I spoke Sunday before flying home Monday morning. I was watching. God had put me on alert.

Since God created Adam and Eve, he has been initiating conversations with humanity, and he often does this with questions. The Bible is scattered with God's questions:

- To Adam and Eve: Where are you? Who told you that you were naked? Have you eaten from the tree that I commanded you not to eat from?[3]
- To Cain: Why are you angry, and why has your countenance fallen? Where is your brother Abel? What have you done?[4]

- To Samuel: How long will you grieve over Saul?[5]
- To Joshua: Why have you fallen on your face? Israel has sinned![6]

Under Joshua's leadership, Jericho was overtaken because the Israelites followed God's direction. When they next went to Ai in their own strength without consulting God, they were soundly defeated—a consequence of hidden sin in the camp. God's questions confront us. How do you answer when you are hiding from him because of disobedience? Do you pass blame like Adam and Eve or hedge with a question like Cain? Or are you truthful and obedient like Samuel and Joshua even though God's instructions may be tough?

Sin has consequences and brings loss, but not without warning. Adam and Eve lost their home in paradise; hard labor and death resulted. Cain became a homeless wanderer. Saul was no longer the anointed king. After sin in the camp was revealed to Joshua, Achan lost his life and that of his family. Yes, sin is costly!

God's questions not only confront us but also alert us and may be preparing us for God-sized assignments, opportunities, or blessings. God said to Moses, "What is that in your hand?"[7] when he was preparing him to lead the children of Israel out of Egypt into the Promised Land. Moses reluctantly obeyed. What's that in *your* hand? Perhaps God is alerting you to a new adventure!

To Elijah God asked, "What are you doing here, Elijah?"[8] A short time before, Elijah had defeated the prophets of Baal and saw fire rain down from heaven as well as showers after a long drought, but now he is hiding, fearful, and depressed after hearing Queen Jezebel's death threats. God is getting ready to send Elijah to anoint new leaders and commission Elisha to succeed him as prophet. What are *you* doing here? Have you had exciting ministries in the past, but you are now sitting on the sidelines, tired and faithless? Is it possible God has a new assignment for you?

God had many questions for Job: "Where were you when I laid the foundations of the earth?" (Job 38:4). "Shall a faultfinder contend with the Almighty?" (Job 40:2, NRSV). And the questioning continues throughout several chapters.[9] God is preparing Job for new blessings, and maybe he's getting you ready for your next blessing.

It is intriguing to me that God asks questions when he already knows the answers. Pay attention to God's questions, for he is preparing you for some revelation.

The New Testament Gospels are filled with questions from the lips of Jesus. "Can all your worries add a single moment to your life?" (Matthew 6:27). "Why do you have so little faith?" (Matthew 6:30). "Do you believe I can make you see?" (Matthew 9:28). "Who do you say that I am?" (Matthew 16:15, NRSV). "What do you want me to do for you?" (Matthew 20:32). "Why are you putting me to the test?" (Matthew 22:18, NRSV). "My God, My God, why have you forsaken me?" (Matthew 27:46, NIV). And many more. Our Lord's questions expose who we really are; they reveal truth about ourselves, our circumstances, and himself.

In my listening time July 24, 2010, God asked me a few questions: "Is my power limited?" "Why do you doubt?" "Why aren't you asking largely—for things only I can do?" I was puzzled by these questions because I thought I *was* asking largely. Even though I had witnessed many miraculous answers to prayer that month, I knew he was stretching me, desiring to enlarge my faith, and preparing me for adventures ahead.

The first week of that month I had gone as the "prayer lady" to a teen camp where twenty-five teens from my church were spending five days along with other students from throughout the state. I had been praying that these teens would witness God's glory revealed in such a way that they could attribute it only to him—not to the dynamic speaker, the gifted praise band, the emotion of the crowd, or any other human source.

Those prayers were answered beyond my greatest, faith-filled expectations. By the end of the week, teens were declaring, "I came to camp to have fun; I had no idea I would encounter God in such a dynamic, life-changing way. I'm returning home transformed. I'll never be the same." One story may give a glimpse of what I witnessed that memorable week.

He appeared at teen camp out of nowhere—or so it seemed. Actually, he arrived at our church parking lot with baggage and signed registration and permission forms, expecting to ride in the vans with our teens. He knew no one at camp; not one of the two hundred fifty campers from across the state knew him. It took weeks to piece together the story of how he even knew about the camp. From the look in his eyes, anyone could see that he was a troubled teen—that is, when you could see his eyes. His countenance remained downcast, with his black hair drooping over his face. His clothing was black, the atmosphere surrounding him bleak—his tormented spirit obvious.

I knew nothing about this last-minute camper until our group meeting Tuesday after the evening chapel service. He sat across the circle from me, and God allowed my eyes and heart to pierce into his very soul. I cried myself to sleep that night praying for this young man to whom I had not spoken one word. I knew nothing about this teen I will call Jay and wondered, "Where did he come from? Why haven't I seen him before? What is his connection with our group?" I awakened, once again sobbing and praying for Jay.

As I began my prayer walk on the campground at daybreak, I called parents of teens asking them to pray with me over the phone and to gather others to pray with them throughout the day. Although the week was filled with many answers to prayer, a highlight was the final night of camp at midnight when another camper, Len, asked Jay if he would like to pray. Jay was ready; they were in the dorm, too engrossed in talking to God to realize they were missing the fireworks finale by the lake!

I learned that fifteen-year-old Jay had visited church only a few times with a friend in fifth grade. Everything about this Christian camp was foreign to him. No doubt it was God-ordained. How else can you explain such a story that has many additional astounding details?

The first time Jay came to church, I was blindsided by an unexpected question. I knew the worship service would be very different from anything he had experienced at camp. He is a musician; the music would be different from the music he creates, plays, and hears. Although we had a talented worship band and choir, the melodies and beat would not be the same as the college band at camp. I stood in the choir and wondered how he would respond.

My position on the platform pointed my vision away from the teen section up front where Jay was sitting with friends he had made at camp. Hands were raised by choir members as well as individuals in the congregation as we sang a joyful hymn. I was singing my heart out, thinking, *Even though this isn't Jay's style of music, it's beautiful; I hope he doesn't tune it out and miss the message.*

Still singing at the top of my voice, hoping Jay was catching the atmosphere of praise, God interrupted my thoughts with this inquiry: *Who are you singing to?* I caught my breath as I turned my focus toward Jesus, whose name I was lifting in song! I recall that question often when I am worshiping.

Yes, God questions; he probes. No doubt his penetrating question will startle you, but take notice, for he is preparing you for some revelation.

I have discovered both through Scripture and in my own personal conversations with God that he welcomes our questions. You may have a few for him today:

- Where are you? How long must I wait?

- What would you have me do in this situation?
- Where are you leading me? Did I hear you correctly?

It is always fitting to ask him, "What do you want to say to me today?" or "What message do you have for me from this passage of scripture?" Ask God if he has anything to say to you from the opening question in the second chapter of the book of James:

> My dear brothers and sisters, how can you claim to have faith in our glorious Lord Jesus Christ if you favor some people over others? (James 2:1).

When I read that question in James, I think of the Jays in my world. When I asked Jay if it was hard for him to ride in a van three hours with people he had never met to attend his first Christian camp, he said, "Yes, I was afraid I wouldn't be accepted. You know, most people don't grin at the way I dress and how I look, so I decided I would spend the week listening to my iPod, texting, and playing technology games."

Someone who knew about the camp told his mom, bought him a Bible to bring, paid his way, made sure he had proper permission forms completed, and he showed up on our church parking lot with an adult confirming that he was permitted to go. What if our adult leaders had refused to let him go because he did not look like the other teens in the van? What if Len had not reached out to befriend him? What if the adults at camp had not loved and prayed for him? What if Jay saw Christians showing favoritism?

James asks a dozen more sobering questions in chapter two. In verse 14 he inquires, "What good is it, dear brothers and sisters, if you say you have faith but don't show it by your actions?" (James 2:14).

He gives examples of faith plus good deeds and emphasizes with a question: "Can't you see that faith without good deeds is useless?" (James 2:20).

In the first chapter of James, his readers are encouraged to ask God for wisdom. When you ask God a question or request wisdom or wonder how to add good deeds to your faith, wait and listen, anticipating an answer—watching for it. It may come in a unique form, and you don't want to miss his answer.

When Paul defended himself to King Agrippa, he recounted the question he heard when he was struck down on the road to Damascus and the answer to his responding question:

We all fell down, and I heard a voice from heaven saying to me in Aramaic, "Saul, Saul, why are you persecuting me? It is useless for you to fight against my will." "Who are you, Lord?" I asked. And the Lord replied, "I am Jesus, the one you are persecuting. Now get to your feet! For I have appeared to you to appoint you as my servant and witness. You are to tell the world what you have seen and what I will show you in the future. And I will rescue you from both your own people and the Gentiles. Yes, I am sending you to the Gentiles to open their eyes, so they may turn from darkness to light and from the power of Satan to God. Then they will receive forgiveness for their sins and be given a place among God's people, who are set apart by faith in me (Acts 26:14-18).

From this example of a dynamic question, it is clear that, like Peter when Jesus asked, "Do you love me?" God was making a shattering revelation to Saul, preparing to transform him into missionary Paul, commissioning him to penetrate the darkness of the world with the message of the Light of the World.

Two thousand-plus years later, men and women still hear the question Jesus posed to Peter: "Do you love me more than these?" (John 21:15) and are commissioned to follow Jesus wherever he leads. All believers, like Paul and Peter, are invited on God-sized adventures to take the light to a sin-darkened world. How will you respond to his request?

Reflections

- What are you expecting God to do through you today?
- Do you expect a miracle?
- What question is God asking you? Just as you want a response from God to your question, he will listen for your answer.
- After you ask God a question, wait, watch, and listen for his answer through Scripture, his still small voice, surrounding circumstances, or surprising avenues.

Scripture

- Reread Acts 26
- John 21
- James 1-2

Memorize James 1:5-6

If you need wisdom, ask our generous God, and he will give it to you. He will not rebuke you for asking. But when you ask him, be sure your faith is in God alone.

Suggestion

Combine several memorization tips from previous chapters.

Reflection Insights

_____

_____

_____

_____

_____

_____

_____

_____

_____

_____

_____

_____

_____

_____

_____

_____

_____

_____

_____

_____

_____

_____

11. SPEAK WORDS OF LIFE

A spoken blessing has power to infuse and reshape a life.

> *Do not let any unwholesome talk come out of your mouths, but only what is helpful for building others up according to their needs, that it may benefit those who listen* (Ephesians 4:29, NIV).

Our words have power to build up or tear down, not only the words we use in sentences that we voice aloud to others, but also those we speak in silent messages to ourselves. Jesus said that what we say comes from the heart.[1] If our heart has been surrendered to God, cleansed by the blood of Jesus, and filled with the Holy Spirit, both our spoken and inaudible words will come from a pure and holy source and will be words of truth and blessing.

Florence Littauer, author of *Silver Boxes*, a book about the power of our words, was visiting a Sunday worship service in a church where she would be speaking to the staff that week. When the pastor spotted her in the audience, he invited her to come forward to say a few words. As she started to rise, he added, "In fact, why don't we have Mrs. Littauer give the children's sermon?"[2]

She had never given a children's sermon and began formulating a plan as she walked down the aisle trailed by all the children. Ephesians 4:29 came to her mind since it was a verse she and her husband, Fred, had taught their children. As the children helped her take the King James Version of the verse apart, they decided that corrupt communication and unwholesome talk meant bad words and that "edify" meant to build up.

One little boy said, "Our words should be like building blocks."[3]

Another added, "And we shouldn't go around and knock other people's blocks down!"[4]

As Florence moved to the last phrase, which says that our words should minister grace, she commented that they should be like presents to be given away. One tiny girl stepped into the aisle and said loudly to the whole congregation, "What she means is that our words should be like little silver boxes with bows on top."[5] That powerful statement prompted Florence to write *Silver Boxes*.

I am a teacher by profession, and my spiritual gift is teaching; therefore, every time I read the part of James 3:1 that says teachers in the church will be judged more strictly, I pause to do a prayerful soul search. I have discovered, however, that every person, no matter the age, is a teacher to someone. We learn from each other by actions we watch and words we hear.

After cautioning teachers, James launched into a discourse on the power of the tongue. He used three visuals to emphasize that although small, the tongue is a mighty force. He compared it to the small bit in the large horse's mouth and a rudder in a huge ship, both with the ability to guide. Then he addressed the tongue's destructive capability, using fire as the image to illustrate the damage that a tiny spark can ignite. So it is with words. Gary Smalley and John Trent in their book *The Blessing* refer to that scripture: "Just like a forest fire, words can burn deeply into our hearts. In fact, the destructive power of fiery words can affect us for the rest of our lives."[6] Proverbs 18:21 says, "The tongue can bring death or life." Our words have the power to lead astray or to guide, to tear down or build up, to deflate or inspire, to discourage or encourage, to damage or renovate, to incite anger or minister grace, to curse or bless, to crush or restore, to destroy a dream or cast a new vision, to defeat or bring hope, to wound or to heal. "Some people make cutting remarks, but the words of the wise bring healing" (Proverbs 12:18). I long for all my words to heal, enrich, benefit, edify, and impart wisdom.

My friend Tina has an amazing ministry bravely speaking blessing and hope into lives that have been manipulated, abused, broken, imprisoned, addicted, and feel helpless to change. She is making a difference and has seen scores of victims forgiven, recovered, restored, and given a fresh start with a renewed outlook.

Tina recalls the day she prayed at the altar of her church, scarred and conflicted by words someone had spoken to her regarding her call to ministry. She poured her heart out to her pastor's wife, who knelt beside her. Tina claimed the new words spoken to her that day: "If God has called you, he will have a place for you to serve." God *did* give Tina a place to serve; she now ministers to women in jail.

Several years later I was invited to speak at Tina's jail services. I went through clearance and was led to the secured area where the ladies gathered to sing and hear God's message. I extended words of hope, telling them stories of Bud[7] and Dorie,[8] who wrote *The Girl Nobody Loved*. Neither Tina nor I could have conceived of all God had in store when he called us into his service. Those words of truth are resounding: "If God has called you, he will have a place for you to serve!" It is truth for you as well, because all God's children are called to glorify him and speak words of life and blessing.

A college student in our church years ago stood in the narthex and paid me a compliment. I was moved by her sweet comment but could sense that she was uncomfortable, especially when she said, "I hope this doesn't sound dorky to you." It didn't; instead, her words touched my heart. I am grateful that this girl half my age pushed herself forward to speak a blessing into my life. If it seems impossible for you to speak words of praise, write them in a note, and hand deliver or mail the blessing.

When Marissa turned thirteen, her parents gave her a blessing celebration, and all the guests wrote blessings in a keepsake book. Her parents and grandparents gave her a spoken blessing. I printed mine for her to keep. Don't let the years go by without depositing a blessing into the lives of those you love or speaking God's love into the ears of a stranger.

The words "God loves you," spoken by a college student who gave her testimony in an orphanage, changed Dorie Van Stone's life. "No one had ever told Dorie that she was loved. Rather, she had been verbally and physically abused by caregivers. When Dorie fell into bed that night, she told God that if he loved her, she wanted to be his girl."[9]

That simple prayer changed Dorie forever. As an adult, she became an artist, author, missionary, pastor's wife, mother, and an internationally known speaker. It is doubtful that the college student who spoke those words of truth, hope, and life in Dorie's orphanage ever knew the impact she made. Every word we speak in the name of Jesus and through the power of the Holy Spirit will bear eternal fruit whether we ever see the evidence of it or not. Watch for opportunities to extend blessings, and speak words of life. Be intentional; formulate a plan.

Lysa TerKeurst and her husband wanted to develop new traditions with their family. They decided to have a Christmas breakfast with a box on the table in which to place cards stating the gifts they planned to give Jesus that year. After the special breakfast Christmas morning, her husband went first, saying that his gift was to each day "look for someone who needs a little of my time, money, or encouragement." He added, "By the end of the year, my life will have touched three hundred sixty-five people for Jesus."

After hearing this, Lysa felt her planned gift was weak, so she said, "Me, too; I want to give the same gift to Jesus."

The children decided that would be their gift also. One day Lysa and her girls were eating lunch at a fast-food restaurant when they noticed a gentleman from their neighborhood eating alone. His wife had recently died. As Lysa greeted him, she felt the nudge that he was her person to bless that day. She invited him to dinner, and for weeks he came to eat with them every Monday night. One evening as he was leaving, he paused on the sidewalk beside the house, then stepped over to a bush that had only one bloom. He tenderly touched the flower, looked at it a moment, then turned to Lysa and said, "Don't miss this!"[10]

These were wise words for a busy mom to hear, challenging words that continue to echo. My challenge: Don't miss an opportunity to speak encouragement, hope, and inspiration while it is still called today,[11] for a spoken blessing has the power to infuse and reshape a life.

Live wisely among those who are not believers, and make the most of every opportunity. Let your conversation be gracious and attractive so that you will have the right response for everyone (Colossians 4:5-6).

"Gentle words are a tree of life" (Proverbs 15:4). Life-giving words:

- God loves you!
- He's here; he's all around you; he's everywhere.
- If God has called you, he will have a place for you to serve.
- "Come to Me all you who are weary and heavy-laden, and I will give you rest."[12]
- It doesn't get any better than this!

- "The truth will set you free."[13]
- You are God's special creation.
- Don't miss this!

Reflections

- Intentionally speak a word of blessing into someone's life each day.

Scripture

- James 3-5
- If you have gotten behind in your recommended Scripture reading, this would be a good time to catch up before moving into the final month of *Simply Rejoicing*.

Memorize Psalm 19:14 (NIV)

May the words of my mouth and this meditation of my heart be pleasing in your sight, LORD, my Rock and my Redeemer.

Suggestion

Meditate on this verse five to ten minutes, and ask God what he is saying to you.

Reflection Insights

BOW AND HONOR THE LORD

I. FIX YOUR GAZE HEAVENWARD

A glimpse of heaven will ignite hope to keep watching.

But Stephen, full of the Holy Spirit, gazed steadily into heaven and saw the glory of God, and he saw Jesus standing in the place of honor at God's right hand. And he told them, "Look, I see the heavens opened and the Son of Man standing in the place of honor at God's right hand!" (Acts 7:55-56).

The final words of Stephen, the first Christian martyr, were words of life, bold and true, but his accusers did not want to hear them.

Then they put their hands over their ears and began shouting. They rushed at him, and dragged him out of the city and began to stone him (Acts 7:57-58).

That was the beginning of a great wave of persecution that swept over the early church in Jerusalem, and the believers were scattered throughout Judea and Samaria; thus, they became witnesses in Jerusalem, Judea, Samaria, and the ends of the earth.[1] The gospel continues to spread today in the face of great opposition.

Problems accompany growth, and the Scripture does not gloss over conflict. Instead, it exposes issues and reports action taken. The solution to the rumblings of discontent among the Greek-speaking believers, who complained about the food distribution to their widows as compared with the Hebrew-speaking believers, was to select seven men who were full of the Holy Spirit and wisdom and give them the responsibility of running the food program.[2]

Stephen, a man full of faith and the Holy Spirit, was one of the seven chosen. The apostles laid hands on these men and prayed for them. "So, God's message continued to spread" (Acts 6:7). And Stephen was one of God's messengers: "Stephen, a man full of God's grace and power, performed amazing miracles and signs among the people" (Acts 6:8).

No one could stand against the wisdom of Stephen and the Spirit with which he spoke,[3] and those who opposed his message began to make false accusations against him. Stephen was arrested and brought before the high council. His faced glowed as he stood and delivered his defense, which began with God's call to Abraham. He summarized the Old Testament that the high priest and these council members knew well and then infuriated them by declaring—

You stubborn people! You are heathen at heart and deaf to the truth. Must you forever resist the Holy Spirit? That's what your ancestors did, and so do you. Name one prophet your ancestors didn't persecute! They even killed the ones who predicted the coming of the Righteous One—the Messiah whom you betrayed and murdered. You deliberately disobeyed God's law, even though you received it from the hands of angels (Acts 7:51-53).

In the midst of the angry mob that shook their fists at him in rage, Stephen gazed into heaven and saw the glory of God with Jesus at his right side (Acts 7:55). Believers are wise to follow Stephen's example and fix their gaze heavenward in the midst of opposition to the gospel.

I was reminded of Stephen at a recent conference when I heard Jennifer Rothchild tell the story of a pastor who was being tortured in a country hostile to Christianity. When the torturers turned to his ten-year-old son, the pastor pleaded with them, "Not my son!" The son shouted, "Papa, don't deny the Lord!" After the angry authorities left, the young boy said to his battered father, "Papa, you didn't deny the Lord!"

Several years later a lady traveled to that country, met the pastor and his son, and heard this story. She asked the boy, now a young teenager, "How did you do it?"

He answered, "If I had looked to the authorities, I couldn't do it, but when I kept my gaze on the Lord, I could do it."

After telling that incredible story, Jennifer said, "I may be blind, but I know where to fix my gaze!"[4] As Paul states in 2 Corinthians, "So we fix our eyes not on what is seen, but on what is unseen, since what is seen is temporary, but what is unseen is eternal" (2 Corinthians 4:18, NIV).

The word "fix" in English carries a diversity of meanings. Mark Buchanan notes, "It means to mend: to *fix* a leaky faucet. It means to fasten: to *fix* a bracket to a shelf. It means to rig, to tamper with, to prearrange: to *fix* the game."[5] In Greek "It simply connotes an intensity of gaze—a determined, attentive searching out."[6] Buchanan continues, "But the range of meanings in our own language is a happy accident. . . . When we fix our hearts and minds on things above, we practice all three things at once: We mend—we *fix* our wayward attention, our inbred distractedness, our myopia; we fasten—we *fix*—that attention to unseen realities; and we rig—we *fix*—things so that, more and more, we glimpse heaven in places and situations where before we saw only shadows and surfaces."[7] Then he adds, "Heaven is meant to be our *fixation* . . . to uncover eternity in our hearts, to recover the hope of forever."[8]

My friend Bonnie has the hope of forever in her heart as she relives in her mind the things she witnessed in a hospital room before her sixteen-year-old son went to be with Jesus. Bonnie called my husband late Saturday night to tell him they were taking her son Carey to the hospital. She told Curtis not to come unless she called him when they got to the emergency room. Curtis headed to the medical center very early Sunday morning. He sensed heaven was near the moment he walked into that all-star baseball pitcher's room.

In a slow, slurred voice Carey said, "Hello, Pastor."

In a few moments he said, "It's Jesus. It's so bright." When Carey sensed his mother was distraught, he comforted her and said, "It's okay, Mom, if it's Jesus' will."

Soon he went into a coma. Approximately nine hundred teens and adults crowed the sanctuary for the memorial service, and thirty-plus years later Carey's classmates still call Bonnie to tell of his impact on their lives. Bonnie recently said that she vividly remembers Carey's calmness and that in spite of her fear, a heavenly atmosphere filled the room.

No eye has seen, what no ear has heard, and what no mind has conceived—the things God has prepared for those who love him (1 Corinthians 2:9, NIV).

Just as a new baby cannot conceive of life outside the mother's womb, we cannot comprehend what heaven will be like. We try to picture it, fumble for words to explain, and get an inkling from those like Carey who see through new eyes. Carey's faith inspires me to continue to fix my gaze heavenward—to watch and listen—and rejoice!

Memories of Ann also give me a glimpse of heaven and cause me to listen with spiritual ears. Ann lay dying in the hospital. Each day when Curtis visited her, she was humming and would ask him, "Pastor, do you hear the music?" He couldn't, but Ann could hear heavenly sounds. Ann, who had suffered hard and long, continued to have a sweet spirit. Her body, racked by pain, had wasted away, but she eagerly awaited seeing her Savior and receiving a transformed, spiritual body that is imperishable.[9]

Our citizenship is in heaven. And we eagerly await a Savior from there, the Lord Jesus Christ, who by the power that enables him to bring everything under his control, will transform our lowly bodies so that they will be like his glorious body (Philippians 3:20-21, NIV).

Ann had fixed her gaze on things unseen and was given a glimpse of what was to come through the music and sounds of heaven. Ann's story prompts me to keep looking up while rejoicing!

Mark Buchanan says our reason for looking up is that as Christians we are dead already; he bases this on Paul's words to the Colossians:

Since you have been raised to new life with Christ, set your sights on the realities of heaven, where Christ sits in the place of honor at God's right hand. Think about the things of heaven, not the things of earth. For you died to this life, and your real life is hidden with Christ in God. And when Christ, who is your life, is revealed to the whole world, you will share in all his glory (Colossians 3:1-4).

Buchanan says,

Christians are dead men walking. We died with Jesus—entered into his saving death, where all the sin that condemned us was done away with. And then he raised us to new life. Christians are not people who one day will be resurrected. We are already walking in the resurrection. We have already been infused with the same Holy Spirit and received the same power that raised Jesus from the grave.[10]

Incredible truth!

Yes, I, who have been resurrected to new life, choose to look heavenward—although earthbound at this time. As I fix my gaze on things unseen and listen expectantly, I await the day when I will no longer attend funerals, suffer, and wipe tears from my eyes.

He will wipe every tear from their eyes, and there will be no more death or sorrow or crying or pain. All these things are gone forever (Revelation 21:4).

John, the beloved disciple, in his old age recorded what he saw and heard in a vision:

> And the one sitting on the throne said, "Look, I am making everything new!" And then he said to me, "Write this down, for what I tell you is trustworthy and true." And he also said, "It is finished! I am the Alpha and Omega—the Beginning and the End. To all who are thirsty I will give freely from the springs of the water of life. All who are victorious will inherit all these blessings, and I will be their God, and they will be my children" (Revelation 21:5-7).

Then John was taken by the Spirit to a high mountain and shown a holy city that shone with the glory of God.[11] John wrote,

> I saw no temple in the city, for the Lord God Almighty and the Lamb are its temple. And the city has no need of sun or moon, for the glory of God illuminates the City, and the Lamb is its light (Revelation 21:22-23).

John clearly stated that nothing evil will be allowed to enter—only those whose names are written in the Lamb's Book of Life.[12]

In the final chapter of Revelation, the Faithful One declares again that he is the Alpha and Omega, the First and the Last, saying,

> Look, I am coming soon, bringing my reward with me to repay all people according to their deeds. . . . I, Jesus, have sent my angel to give you this message for the churches. . . . I am the bright morning star. . . . Yes, I am coming soon! (Revelation 22:12-20).

The Old Testament pointed to the coming of the Messiah; the first four books of the New Testament tell of his life on earth; the remaining books give accounts of what happened after his resurrection; and the final two chapters point us heavenward to where the Alpha and Omega, the Beginning and the End, waits and intercedes for us in the place of honor at God's right hand.

And until you come, Lord Jesus, we will fix our gaze on you:

Fixing our eyes on Jesus, the pioneer and perfecter of faith. For the joy set before him he endured the cross, scorning its shame, and sat down at the right hand of the throne of God. Consider him who endured such opposition from sinful men, so that you will not grow weary and lose heart (Hebrews 12:2-3, NIV).

I pray that I will not grow weary and lose heart as I continue my earthly journey heavenward. I give thanks for all the glimpses of God at work in the world around me that he has revealed, and I know he has more for me to witness as I continue watching and rejoicing while waiting.

Reflections

- Record in your journal the glimpses of God you have witnessed today.
- What is your plan for being more alert to what God is doing around you?

Scripture

- Revelation 21-22

Memorize John 14:1-3

Don't let your hearts be troubled. Trust in God, and trust also in me. There is more than enough room in my Father's home. If this were not so, would I have told you that I am going to prepare a place for you? When everything is ready, I will come and get you, so that you will always be with me where I am.

Suggestion

Create your own plan or choose one that works best for you.

Reflection Insights

_____
_____
_____
_____
_____
_____
_____
_____
_____
_____
_____
_____
_____
_____
_____
_____
_____
_____
_____
_____
_____

II. CONCLUSION—WATCH WITH WIDE-EYED WONDER

A vision of his glory will send you forth rejoicing!

He took me in the Spirit to a great, high mountain, and he showed me the holy city, Jerusalem, descending out of heaven from God. It shone with the glory of God and sparkled like a precious stone—like jasper as clear as crystal (Revelation 21:10-11).

I was an infant when the doctor told my parents I would need to have eye surgery someday. The day I received my first pair of wire-rimmed glasses, I was a preschooler—barely out of the toddler category. Yes, I vividly remember that next morning when I begged to go outside to play with my older sister and neighborhood friends—without my glasses. Mother gave in reluctantly and said I could play without them for only thirty minutes. Although I stretched the time as long as I could before going indoors, I soon wore them faithfully, because they improved my vision drastically. Four surgeries and numerous pairs of glasses and contacts later, I can attest that corrective vision can change your view of everything.

As great as eye surgeons, ophthalmologists, optometrists, opticians, and visual technicians may be, they are powerless to correct or modify one's spiritual vision. That comes from the Word of God and other means the Holy Spirit uses to awaken us. A word from God can cause us to forever view a person, circumstance, or idea through different lenses. Seeing through his eyes changes everything.

This morning in our Pentecost Sunday worship service with hundreds of others, I asked God to open the eyes of my heart. Included in that request, I added Ann Voskamp's prayer: "O Lord, open the eyes of my heart, the eyes of my hands, the eyes of my mouth, the eyes of my feet. I long to be all eye."[1] Ann declared, "I want to be like the cherubim, with 'eyes all over their bodies, including their hands, their backs, and their wings' (Ezekiel 10:12). I want to be like Moses, who 'kept right on going because he kept his eyes on the one who is invisible' (Hebrews 11:27). *That is what makes us persevere through a life: to see him who is invisible!*"[2] I saw him, the Invisible One, this morning in corporate worship as we sang hymns and lifted our praise to God, as Scripture was read, as the pastor reminded us that every Sunday is Pentecost, because when we gather to worship God and lift up the name of Jesus, his Spirit is present and outpoured afresh!

Throughout this rejoicing adventure of watching to see God at work in my world, I have traced the Christian calendar in my own journey. I began writing *Simply Rejoicing* during Advent, the season before Christmas when Christians remember those of old who watched for the coming of the promised Messiah and believers are reminded that we today are watching with expectation and hope for his return. I have continued writing throughout the celebrations of the Christian calendar: Christmas, Epiphany, Lent, Holy Week, Easter, and Pentecost Sunday today.

"Seven weeks after Easter, we remember that first Christian Pentecost, when the Lord Jesus baptized his apostles in the Holy Spirit. So it is by the Spirit that we confess, 'Jesus Christ is Lord,' and it is by the Spirit that we say, 'Abba, Father.' Now all may be filled with the Spirit who is Love."[3]

Now I move forward into the final season of the church year, called the season of Trinity, which begins on Trinity Sunday one week after Pentecost Sunday and will continue until Advent begins again. Thomas Noble wrote, "Here we recognize that the whole story we have been tracing, the story of Jesus, is the story of our Triune God. For it is God as Father, who, out of love, sent God as Son, Love Incarnate, and poured out his Spirit, who is Love to perfect his people in Love."[4]

Voskamp portrays an image of Love Incarnate: "Jesus lies over a heart and his transparency burns the cataracts off the soul."[5] I echo her words that follow:

> The only way to see God manifested in the world around is with the eyes of Jesus within. God within is the One seeing God without. God is both the object of my seeing and subject who does the act of all real seeing, the Word lens the inner eye wears. To sit in the theater of God and see his glory crack the dark, to open the eyes of my heart to see the fountain of his grace—thousands of gifts—I have to split heart open to more and more of Jesus. Who can split open the eyelids but Jesus? He tears the veil to the Holy of Holies, gives me the only seeing I have. I have been lost and now I am found and I sing it softly. . . "Be thou my vision, O Lord of my heart . . . "[6]

This is my closing refrain: With the blind beggar, my desire is to see![7]

- To see God's glory—for I was made for his glory and to glorify him;

- To behold miracles all around me wrought by the Holy Spirit—for his Spirit has been poured out on me, and he lives within;
- I want to see Jesus—for he is my healer, the eye surgeon of my heart, my Savior and coming King.

Thus, I will pray unceasingly with eyes wide open to the Triune God, Father, Son, and Holy Spirit. Amen.

Reflections

- Spend a few moments sitting quietly in his presence.
- Before the end of the year, reread portions or all your journal entries recorded during this year of simply rejoicing.

Scripture

Ask God to guide where you are to read in his Word as you conclude this watching-with-rejoicing pilgrimage.

Memorize

Review previously memorized verses.

Reflection Insights

_____

_____

_____

_____

_____

_____

_____

_____

_____

_____

_____

_____

_____

_____

_____

_____

_____

_____

_____

_____

_____

_____

_____

_____

BENEDICTION

I commit *Simply Rejoicing* to the Father, Son, and Holy Spirit. It is my prayer that all who read its pages will behold your creation, heavenly Father, and see through your eyes and heart the world around them and everyone you choose to cross their path. Give them insight into your Word, watchfulness in today's activities, and farsightedness that focuses on your vision for the journey ahead.

My heart desires that the dear ones turning these pages will exalt you, precious Jesus, in everything they do and say, and may their lips praise you for your blessings and saving grace. May they turn their eyes toward you and fix their gaze on the One and Only, Faithful and True, who sits at the right hand of the Father interceding for them.

Breath of Heaven, you who breathed life into the one who holds this book, will you breathe afresh on him or her, cleansing, purifying, infilling for the work you have ordained. Bring comfort, and make your presence known to this committed one as he or she simply watches to see God at work.

Holy God, Three in One, you are here! You are all around us! You are everywhere! I commit this book to you.

I will exalt you, my God and King,
and praise your name forever and ever.
I will praise you every day;
yes, I will praise you forever.

Great is the LORD! He is most worthy of praise!
  No one can measure his greatness.
Let each generation tell its children of your mighty acts;
  let them proclaim your power.
I will meditate on your majestic, glorious splendor
  and your wonderful miracles.
Your awe-inspiring deeds will be on every tongue;
  I will proclaim your greatness.
Everyone will share the story of your wonderful goodness;
  they will sing with joy about your righteousness.
The LORD is merciful and compassionate,
  slow to get angry and filled with unfailing love.
The LORD is good to everyone.
  He showers compassion on all his creation.
All of your works will thank you, LORD,
  and your faithful followers will praise you.
They will speak of the glory of your kingdom;
  they will give examples of your power.
They will tell about your mighty deeds
  and about the majesty and glory of your reign.
For your kingdom is an everlasting kingdom.
  You rule throughout all generations.
The LORD always keeps his promises;
  he is gracious in all he does.
The LORD helps the fallen
  and lifts those bent beneath their loads.
The eyes of all look to you in hope;
  you give them their food as they need it.
When you open your hand,
  you satisfy the hunger and thirst of every living thing.

the LORD is righteous in everything he does;
>
> he is filled with kindness.

The LORD is close to all who call on him,
>
> yes, to all who call on him in truth.

He grants the desires of those who fear him;
>
> he hears their cries for help and rescues them.

The LORD protects all those who love him,
>
> but he destroys the wicked.

I will praise the LORD,
>
> and may everyone on earth bless his holy name,
>
>> forever and ever (Psalm 145).

Amen!

NOTES

Foreword

1. Patsy Lewis, *Simply Praying* (Kansas City: Beacon Hill Press of Kansas City, 2006), 15.

First Month—Part I

1. Calvin Miller, *The Path of Celtic Prayer* (Downer's Grove, Ill.: Intervarsity Press, 2007), 48.

2. Robert E. Coleman, *The Heart of the Gospel* (Grand Rapids: Baker Books, 2011), 14.

3. Matthew 3:16-17.

4. Matthew 28:19.

5. John 14-17.

6. Coleman, *The Heart of the Gospel*, 16.

7. Ibid.

First Month—Part II

1. Mark Batterson, *The Circle Maker* (Grand Rapids: Zondervan Publishing House, 2011), 13.

2. Ibid.

3. Ibid., 14.

4. Ibid., 186.

5. Ibid., 179-86.

Second Month—Part I

1. Luke 4:2, 13.

2. Luke 5:29.

3. Elmer L. Towns, *Fasting for Spiritual Breakthrough* (Ventura, Calif.: Regal Books, 1996), 13.

4. Ibid., 15.

5. Ibid., 14.

6. Ibid.

7. Lysa TerKeurst, *Made to Crave* (Grand Rapids: Zondervan Publishing House, 2010), 19.

Second Month—Part II

1. Mark 1:17; John 21:22.
2. Matthew 10:2; Mark 3:16; Luke 6:14.
3. John 1:42.
4. Matthew 10:1-4; Mark 6:7-10; Luke 9:1-2.
5. Matthew 14:28-33.
6. Mark 5:35-43.
7. Matthew 17:1-13; Mark 9:2-13; Luke 9:28-36.
8. Luke 22:61-62.
9. Matthew 28:18-19.
10. Acts 1:15.
11. Acts 2.
12. Acts 3:19.
13. Acts 4:4.
14. Acts 9:36-42.
15. Acts 10.
16. Patsy Lewis, "Can You Relate?" *Holiness Today* 15:1 (January-February 2013): 34-35.
17. Linda Boyette et al., *Living in the Overflow* (Wilmore, Ky.: Titus Women, 2012), 7.
18. Ibid., 8.
19. Ibid., 8-9.

Third Month—Part I

1. Joyce Williams, *God Sightings* (Kansas City: Beacon Hill Press of Kansas City, 2009), 22-24.
2. Batterson, *The Circle Maker*, 126.
3. Ann Voskamp, *One Thousand Gifts* (Grand Rapids: Zondervan Publishing House, 2012), 20.
4. Ibid., 21.
5. Ibid.
6. Ibid., 22.
7. Acts 9:8.
8. Acts 8:3.
9. Acts 9:1.
10. Galatians 5:25.
11. Batterson, *The Circle Maker*, 122.

Third Month—Part II

1. Acts 16:1-5.

2. Real persons, but real names not used.

3. Hal Perkins, *If Jesus Were a Parent* (n.p., 2006), 87.

4. Ibid., 99.

5. Ibid.

6. John 4:35.

Fourth Month—Part I

1. Titus women's Ministry with Patsy Lewis, *Lydia Leader's Guide—Incredible Power in Praying Women* (Wilmore, Ky.: Francis Asbury Society, 2011), 6.

2. Ibid., 8.

Fourth Month—Part II

1. Philippians 1:6.

2. Dorinda Biggs, Patsy Lewis, and Jo Apple, "The Great I Am" *Enter His Rest,* CD (Hip and Holy, a division of HCT Media, LLC, 2011), track 2. Used by permission.

Fifth Month—Part I

1. 1 Thessalonians 1:6.

2. John 3:15.

3. Acts 27-28.

4. 1 Thessalonians 2:12.

5. 1 Thessalonians 5:23, NIV.

6. 1 Thessalonians 2:12.

7. 1 Thessalonians 5:5.

8. 1 Thessalonians 5:6.

9. 1 Thessalonians 5:21.

10. Mark Buchanan, *Things Unseen* (Sisters, Oreg.: Multnomah Publishers, 2002), 157.

11. Coleman, *The Heart of the Gospel*, 227.

Fifth Month—Part II.

1. Patsy Lewis, *Come to the Fire Testimonies* (Leawood, Kans.: Come to the Fire, 2010), 54-56. Used by permission.

2. Ibid., 57-65. Used by permission.

3. Ibid. Used by permission.

4. Ibid. Used by permission.

5. Romans 6:11.

6. 1 Corinthians 15:58, NIV.

Sixth Month—Part I

1. Acts 18:18-22.

2. Acts 19:8-10.

3. Ephesians 1:15-20.

4. Ephesians 3:12.

5. Ephesians 4:1-6.

6. Ephesians 4:29-30.

Sixth Month—Part II

1. Acts 8:1-4.

2. Acts 8:26-40.

3. John 13:34, NIV.

4. Acts 1:8.

5. Ibid.

Seventh Month—Part I

1. Jim Cymbala with Stephen and Amanda Sorenson, *When God's People Pray* (Grand Rapids: Zondervan Publishing House, 2007), 15.

2. Danny Velasco, *The Brooklyn Tabernacle Choir Live . . . This Is Your House*, CD, 2003, CD testimony, track 5.

3. Ibid.

4. Ibid.

5. Jim Cymbala, *When God's People Pray* (Grand Rapids: Zondervan Publishing House, 2007), DVD.

6. Ibid.

Seventh Month—Part II

1. Todd Phillips, *Spiritual CPR* (Colorado Springs: Cook Communication Ministries, 2005), 65-66.

2. Ibid., 23.

3. Ibid., 72.

4. Ibid., 215-18.

5. *The Brooklyn Tabernacle Choir Live. . . . This Is Your House,* track 5.

Eighth Month—Part I

1. Linda Mintle, *I Love My Mother, But . . .* (Eugene, Ore.: Harvest House Publishers, 2004), 7.

2. Lewis, *Come to the Fire Testimonies*, 66-69. Used by permission.

3. Ibid., 69-71. Used by permission.

4. Colossians 3:12-17.

Eighth Month—Part II

1. Nancy Leigh DeMoss, *Lies Women Believe* (Chicago: Moody Publishers, 2001), 249.

2. Ibid., 249-51.

3. Colossians 1:9-10.

4. Colossians 1:11-14.

Ninth Month—Part I

1. Patsy Lewis, *Simply Listening* (Kansas City: Beacon Hill Press of Kansas City, 2009), 165.

2. John 1:39.

3. John 1:40-42.

4. John 1:44-46.

5. Luke 19:5.

6. Acts 16:15.

7. Acts 28:8-9.

8. Acts 28:17.

9. Acts 28:30.

10. Acts 28:24.

Ninth Month—Part II

1. Mark 1:17.

Tenth Month—Part I

1. Marilyn Feinberg, *The Sacred Echo* (Grand Rapids: Zondervan Publishing House, 2008), 38.

2. Ibid.

3. Luke 24:27.

4. Mark Batterson, *Soul Print* (Colorado Springs: Multnomah Books, 2012), 3.

5. Ibid.

6. Ibid., 117.

7. John 1:14.

8. John 14:6.

9. Stormie Omartian, *The Power of a Praying Parent* (Eugene, Oreg.: Harvest House Publishers, 2006), 128-29.

10. Ibid.

11. Ibid., 113-18.

12. Ibid., 116-17.

13. Batterson, *The Circle Maker*, 93.

Tenth Month—Part II

1. A. Paget Wilkes, *Sanctification*, 11th ed. (London: Headley Brothers, 1947), 27-39.

2. Ibid., 34.

3. Ibid.

4. Ibid., 34-35.

5. Ibid., 35.

6. Ibid.

7. Ibid., 38-39.

8. Ibid., 38.

9. Ibid.

10. Dennis F. Kinlaw, *The Mind of Christ* (Nappanee, Ind.: Francis Asbury Press of Evangelical Publishing House, 1998), 28.

11. Ibid., 28-29.

12. Ibid., 6.

13. Ibid., 19.

Eleventh Month—Part I

1. John 21:15-16.

2. Matthew 26:36-45.

3. Genesis 3:9-11, NIV.

4. Genesis 4:6-10.

5. 1 Samuel 16:1.

6. Joshua 7:10-11.

7. Exodus 4:2.

8. 1 Kings 19:9, 13.

9. Job 38-41.

Eleventh Month—Part II

1. Luke 6:45

2. Florence Littauer, *Silver Boxes* (Dallas: Word Publishing, 1989), 1.

3. Ibid., 3.

4. Ibid.

5. Ibid.

6. Gary Smalley and John Trent, *The Blessing* (Nashville: Thomas Nelson Publishers, 1986), 51.

7. See chapter 4.

8. Lewis, *Simply Listening*, 185-86.

9. Ibid.

10. Lysa TerKeurst, told at Extraordinary Women's Conference, Tulsa, Okla., March 2012.

11. Hebrews 3:13.

12. Matthew 11:28-30, NASB.

13. John 8:32.

Twelfth Month—Part I

1. Acts 1:8.

2. Acts 6:1-4.

3. Acts 6:10.

4. Jennifer Rothchild, told at Extraordinary Women's Conference, March 3, 2012.

5. Buchanan, *Things Unseen*, 11.

6. Ibid., 12.

7. Ibid.

8. Ibid.

9. 1 Corinthians 15:42-56.

10. Buchanan, *Things Unseen*, 167.

11. Revelation 21:10-11.

12. Revelation 21:27.

Twelfth Month—Part II

1. Voskamp, *One Thousand Gifts*, 115.

2. Ibid.

3. Thomas A. Noble. "Through the Year with the Lord," *Holiness Today* 14:2 (March-April, 2012): 25.

4. Ibid.

5. Voskamp, *One Thousand Gifts*, 116-117.

6. Ibid.

7. Luke 18:41.

BIBLIOGRAPHY

Batterson, Mark. *The Circle Maker*. Grand Rapids: Zondervan Publishing House, 2011.

———. *Soul Print*. Colorado Springs: Multnomah Books, 2011.

Boyette, Linda, et al. *Living in the Overflow*. Wilmore, Ky.: Titus Women, a ministry of the Francis Asbury Society, 2012.

Buchanan, Mark. *Things Unseen*. Sisters, Oreg.: Multnomah Publishers, 2002.

Coleman, Robert E. *The Heart of the Gospel*. Grand Rapids: Baker Books, 2011.

Cymbala, Jim. *When God's People Pray*. Grand Rapids: Zondervan Publishing House, 2007. DVD.

Cymbala, Jim with Stephen Sorenson and Amanda Sorenson. *When God's People Pray*. Grand Rapids: Zondervan Publishing House, 2007.

Demoss, Nancy Leigh. *Lies Women Believe*. Chicago: Moody Publishers, 2001.

Feinberg, Marilyn. *The Sacred Echo*. Grand Rapids: Zondervan Publishing House, 2008.

Kinlaw, Dennis F. *The Mind of Christ*. Nappanee, Ind.: Francis Asbury Press of Evangelical Publishing House, 1998.

Lewis, Patsy. "Can You Relate?" *Holiness Today* 15, no. 1 (January-February 2013): 34-35.

———. *Come to the Fire Testimonies*. Leawood, Kans.: Come to the Fire, 2012.

———. *Simply Listening*. Kansas City: Beacon Hill Press of Kansas City, 2009.

———. *Simply Praying*. Kansas City: Beacon Hill Press of Kansas City, 2006.

Littauer, Florence. *Silver Boxes*. Dallas: Word Publishing Company, 1989.

Miller, Calvin. *The Path of Celtic Prayer*. Downer's Grove, Ill.: Intervarsity Press, 2007.

Mintle, Linda. *I Love My Mother, But . . . .* Eugene, Oreg.: Harvest House Publishers, 2004.

Noble, Thomas A. "Through the Year with the Lord". *Holiness Today* 14, no. 2 (March-April 2012): 25.

Omartian, Stormie. *The Power of the Praying Parent*. Eugene, Oreg.: Harvest House Publishers, 2006.

Perkins, Hal. *If Jesus Were a Parent*. n.p., 2006.

Phillips, Todd. *Spiritual CPR*. Colorado Springs: Cook Communication Ministries, 2005.

Smalley, Gary and John Trent. *The Blessing*. Nashville: Thomas Nelson Publishers, 1986.

TerKeurst, Lysa. *Made to Crave*. Grand Rapids: Zondervan Publishing House, 2010.

Titus Women's Ministry with Patsy Lewis. *Lydia Leader's Guide—Incredible Power in Praying Women*. Wilmore, Ky.: Francis Asbury Society, 2011.

Towns, Elmer L. *Fasting for Spiritual Breakthrough*. Ventura, Calif.: Regal Books, 1996.

Velasco, Danny. *The Brooklyn Tabernacle Choir Live . . . This Is Your House*. 2003. CD.

Voskamp, Ann. *One Thousand Gifts*. Grand Rapids: Zondervan Publishing House, 2012.

Wilkes, A. Paget. *Sanctification*. 11th ed. London: Headley Brothers, 1947.

Williams, Joyce. *God Sightings*. Kansas City: Beacon Hill Press of Kansas City, 2009.